AMERICAN
MONROE

AMERICAN MONROE

The Making of a Body Politic

S. PAIGE BATY

University of California Press

Berkeley Los Angeles London

Photo on page ii: detail of photo on page 86.
UPI/Bettman.
Photo on page vi: Jon Miller.

University of California Press
Berkeley and Los Angeles, California

University of California Press, Ltd.
London, England

Library of Congress Cataloging-in-
Publication Data

Baty, S. Paige, 1961–
    American Monroe : the making of a body
politic / S. Paige Baty.
        p.   cm.
    Includes bibliographical references and
index.
    ISBN 0-520-08805-0 (alk. paper).—ISBN 0-
520-08806-9 (pbk. : alk. paper)
    1. Monroe, Marilyn, 1926–1962—
Criticism and interpretation.   2. Popular
culture—United States.   3. Motion
picture—Social aspects—United States.
I. Title.
PN 2287.M69B38   1995
791.43'028'092—dc20   94-10258

Printed in the United States of America
9   8   7   6   5   4   3   2   1
The paper used in this publication meets
the minimum requirements of American
National Standard for Information
Sciences—Permanence of Paper for Printed
Library Materials, ANSI Z39.48-1984.

This book is for my teacher and friend John H. Schaar.

When she first came to me I was amazed at the startling sensitivity which she possessed and which had remained fresh and undimmed, struggling to express itself despite the life to which she had been subjected.

**Lee Strasberg,
his eulogy at Marilyn's funeral**

She looked like any other baby that I delivered. She was the same as the rest.

Dr. Beerman

Marilyn was involved in something that went way beyond Hoffa—way beyond her affair with Robert Kennedy. . . . The legacy and heritage of the Kennedy family was involved. That must not be destroyed—the thinking went. And a silly little blonde movie star doesn't mean a thing on a national scope.

**Ray Strait,
quoted in *Marilyn: The Last Take***

Marilyn Monroe stared back at me in 1969, these words printed on the face of her burial crypt. Yes, she was now in there behind the marble slab. But in there, too, were the remains of Marilyn Miller (her name by her marriage to the great American playwright, Arthur Miller), Marilyn DiMaggio (by her marriage to the American baseball legend, Joe DiMaggio), Jean Norman (a name she had used on a magazine cover, while still a model), Norma Jean Dougherty (her name by her marriage to "Jimmie"), and, of course, the real occupant of the ːpace I now stood before, Norma Jeane Mortenson. All of them were finally at rest.

**Jim Haspiel,
Marilyn's "number one" fan**

Vladik's passion carried over into the army. Ordered to decorate the base canteen, he painted life-size pictures of heroic peasant women, all of them with Marilyn's face—and nobody noticed. Then, using the army's own art supplies, he began to experiment on himself.

***People* magazine,
about Russian Marilyn impersonator
Vladik Mamyshev**

Contents

Acknowledgments

I would like to thank Vivian Sobchack for her considerable efforts with this book. She has been a valuable reader, mentor, friend, and model of professional excellence. I would also like to thank Michael Rogin for his brilliant reading and suggested revisions of this text, as well as for the model he provides as thinker and writer. Much of the inspiration for this book is derived from his work on American political culture. I would like to thank William Connolly, who read this book in manuscript form for his *Contestations* series with Cornell Press. His comments were exceptional, and many strengths in the project are thanks to his careful editing skills. Also extensive thanks to James Der Derian, who read the book for the Connolly series, and who made a number of excellent critical suggestions for revisions.

I would like to thank my teachers at the University of California at Santa Cruz. Michael Cowan was an invaluable reader of earlier versions of this text, and continues to provide intellectual and personal inspiration. Peter Euben was an important teacher of political thought, who provided interesting counterpositions to journeys I made in political cultural studies. John H. Schaar, to whom this book is dedicated, taught me a great deal about American political culture, and even more about the meaning of being a scholar and teacher. I continue to learn from him. Hayden White provided close readings of versions of this work, and has been a consistently fine teacher, mentor, advisor, and model of academic excellence. Donna Haraway commented on earlier versions of this work, and contributed to the formation of my ideas in feminist political thought.

My colleagues Mark Reinhardt, Russ Castronovo, and Steve Rugare read versions of this text and have greatly assisted in the realization of this project. I have been honored to teach with Mark Reinhardt at Williams College. I could not ask for a more generous and intellectually stimulating colleague: our continuing conversations inform all of my work. Steve Rugare in particular worked very hard with me on earlier versions of this work. He consistently provided keen insights into processes of political cultural life. My colleagues Jana Sawicki and Karen Swann have given productive and substantial input into this text. Karen Swann's close readings of each chapter were fundamental to the revision process, and the realization of the book as a whole.

I would also like to thank the Williams College Francis Oakley Humanities Center and its director Jean Berny Bucky for financial assistance, and the opportunity to participate in seminars with colleagues such as Shawn Rosenheim, Mark Reinhardt, Karen Swann, Jana Sawicki, Jeanne Bergman, Helga Druxes, Chris Waters, Scott Wong, and others who have all given generously in suggestions regarding the manuscript. Raymond Baker provided support for this project. I would also like to thank Williams College for continued intellectual and financial support in terms of grants and leave monies. The Harvard Faculty Mellon Foundation and its director Dr. Richard Hunt provided financial and intellectual support while I revised this project during a leave year at Harvard.

I would like to thank Alice Jardine for useful comments on this work, and conversations on feminist thought. I would like to heartily thank Linda and Hartley Shearer, with whom I am collaborating on the 1997 Williams College Museum of Art exhibition to accompany this text. Their vision has helped to make possible the realization of visual and material versions of the written text.

A few students have made valuable contributions to this text. Jose Marquez read the entire manuscript, had numerous conversations with me about the work, and acted as a research assistant in the final stages of revision. Kirsten Hudson read earlier versions of this manuscript and provided insightful criticisms. Donna Murch worked with me on sections of the book while she was my Ford Mellon advisee.

All books are the result of collaborations, and this is true of *American Monroe*. The professional staff I've been honored to work with at the University of California Press greatly improved this work. My editors at the University of California Press have worked extensively on this project. Naomi Schneider has provided support throughout this project, giving me the space and encouragement I needed to complete the text. I would like to thank in particular my editor William Murphy, with whom I have had extended conversations about the content and form of *American Monroe*. He is the sort of editor one hopes for, providing insight, encouragement, and substantive intellectual contributions throughout the revision process. I continue to learn from William Murphy as a thinker, reader, advisor, and friend. Scott Norton's editorial work was fundamental to the realization of this book. His revisions evidenced grace, intelligence, and skill, and I am deeply appreciative of his efforts. Project editor Tony Hicks oversaw the production of this text, and made valuable suggestions for revision. Designer Nola Burger helped to envision the text, realizing the material textual body of *American Monroe*.

Finally, I would like to thank Gavin Bart for all of his work on this manuscript, and for the friendship, love, and humor he so willingly provides. In him I have found my audience. My mother Pat Baty, my brother Charles Baty, my sisters Kate and Laurel Baty, and my friends Molly McGavern and Leslie Fellows have provided support throughout this project. Anything good in this endeavor is largely due to the friends and colleagues I have thanked; any weaknesses and shortcomings are my own.

Paige Baty

Store interior, Los Angeles. Photo by Jon Miller.

What a jolt to the dream life of the nation that the angel died of an overdose. Whether calculated suicide by barbiturates or accidental suicide by losing count of how many barbiturates she had already taken, or an end even more sinister, no one was able to say. Her death was covered over with ambiguity even as Hemingway's was exploded into horror, and as the deaths and spiritual disasters of the decade of the Sixties came one by one to the American Kings and Queens, as Jack Kennedy was killed, and Bobby, and Martin Luther King, as Jackie Kennedy married Aristotle Onassis and Teddy Kennedy went off the bridge at Chappaquiddick, so the decade that began with Hemingway as the monarch of American arts ended with Andy Warhol as its regent, and the ghost of Marilyn's death gave a lavender edge to that dramatic design of the Sixties which seemed in retrospect to have done nothing so much as to bring Richard Nixon to the threshold of imperial power.

Norman Mailer

There's a broad with a future behind her.

Constance Bennett

Introduction

Marilyn Monroe is beautifully preserved years after her death. She is imprinted and displayed on T-shirts, calendars, postcards, ashtrays, soap dishes, and ceramic mugs. She is suggested by diamonds, signified by blondes. She is impersonated by rock stars, fans, and other actors and actresses. She graces the cover of *A Dictionary of 20th Century Biography*, and also boasts her own encyclopedic text—*The Unabridged Marilyn: Her Life from A to Z*—devoted exclusively to the details of her life and work.[1] She appears on a bottle of wine—Marilyn Merlot—and has been

---

1. Asa Briggs, consultant ed., *A Dictionary of 20th Century World Biography* (Oxford: Oxford University Press, 1991); Randall Riese and Neal Hitchens, *The Unabridged Marilyn: Her Life from A to Z* (New York: Congdon and Weed,

the inspiration for a number of songs, including Elton John's famous "Candle In the Wind."[2] She has been made into earrings and neckties; she has been sold as paper dolls and figurines.[3] She has been the subject of repeated *Life* retrospectives.[4] Her old friends and associates appear frequently on television talk shows to discuss the "real Marilyn," and new books on Marilyn appear several times a year.[5] It appears that we as a culture cannot forget Marilyn Monroe, so we make her up again and again.

1987). Whereas *A Dictionary of 20th Century World Biography* encapsulates the lives of hundreds of subjects, *The Unabridged Marilyn* is devoted exclusively to Marilyn's life as encapsulated subject. *The Unabridged Marilyn* remembers its subject in alphabetized entries that detail her roles in films, the products she endorsed, the homes in which she lived, the stores in which she shopped, the men that she married, the doctors from whom she sought treatment, the hotels in which she slept, the foods she ate, and so on. In this text, the remembered Marilyn is reorganized into a user-friendly format that makes her easily accessible to the reader in a sound-byte fashion. Life as abbreviated encyclopedia.

2. "Candle in the Wind," written by Bernie Taupin, appeared on Elton John's 1973 hit album *Goodbye Yellow Brick Road*. It was rereleased and climbed the charts again in 1991, accompanied by what became a popular video. In the song, a fan says good-bye to "Norma Jean," mourning her death, her exploitation, and the fact that he never had a chance to meet her. In the 1991 video, Marilyn has a chance to "say good-bye" herself: the video features a number of documentary images of the star waving. In these rememberings of Marilyn, mourning becomes electronic, circulating through culture in media that mix nostalgia, simulation, and entertainment.

3. Tom Tierney, *Marilyn Monroe Paper Dolls* (Mineola: Dover Publications Inc., 1979).

4. *Life* cover stories on Marilyn Monroe after her death began with the August 17, 1962, retrospective issue. A second appeared on Aug. 7, 1964, and a third on September 8, 1972, followed by others in October of 1981, August of 1982, July of 1983, May of 1986, the Fall (50th Anniversary) Issue in 1986, April of 1987, and August of 1992, the latest as of this writing.

   Life can be read as the paradigmatic narrative surface on which American cultural consciousness is writ large. From its oversized format to its panoramic insistence on the visual incorporation of culture, *Life*'s photogeneric depiction of America is perfectly suited to Marilyn's remembered forms.

5. Television shows that have focused upon Marilyn include "Marilyn Monroe— What Really Happened?" *Geraldo,* November 10, 1988, with guests such as Marilyn's alleged ex-husband Robert Slatzer; "Marilyn Monroe and Her Se-

This book is an examination of some of the ways that Marilyn has been remembered since her death in 1962.[6] In the years that have passed since Marilyn's death, she has increasingly been understood as one of the first casualties of the 1960s. Though allegations of a conspiracy involving the Kennedys and the mob in Marilyn's death were controversial when Mailer raised them in his 1973 *Marilyn,* similar conspiracy theories have been widely circulated in the mass media of the 80s and

crets—What She Knew," *Donahue,* July 1990, with authors Anthony Summers and Gloria Steinem; and "Peter Lawford, the Kennedys and Marilyn Monroe," *Sally Jesse Raphael,* November 23, 1988. By my count, to date there have been over seventy books devoted exclusively to Marilyn Monroe. Lucy Freeman, *Why Norma Jean Killed Marilyn Monroe: A Psychological Portrait* (Mamaroneck, N.Y.: Hastings House, 1992), mentions that eighty-five books have been written on Marilyn. Riese and Hitchens include an extensive bibliography in their *Unabridged Marilyn,* in which they list forty-eight books focusing exclusively on Marilyn. A number of books have been written since the "encyclopedia's" publication in 1987, such as Graham McCann's academic and biographical study, *Marilyn Monroe* (New Brunswick, N.J.: Rutgers University Press, 1988); Janice Anderson's essays accompanying photographs in *Marilyn Monroe* (London: Ivy Leaf, 1991); Susan Strasberg's personal recollection *Marilyn and Me: Sisters, Rivals, Friends* (New York: Warner Books, 1992); Sam Stagg's novel *MMII: The Return of Marilyn Monroe* (New York: Donald Fine, 1991); and Donald Spoto's "refutation" of other 1980s conspiracy theories in *Marilyn Monroe: The Biography* (New York: HarperCollins, 1993). This is only a partial list: I refer to a number of other recently published texts throughout this book. Books in which Marilyn has been remembered range in form and style from classical biography to fictionalized biography, from photographic collection to personal recollection.

6. As such, it is a schizophrenic text, and this is reflected in the voices of its author. I have been listening for some time to the voices of those who have made the goddess, the chroniclers of mass-mediated immortality. What I have heard is the static of the airwaves, something that runs interference over the story that is told again and again. This listening has been the act of making Marilyn, and it has meant living with her, or the version of her I was writing. Everybody's Marilyn is different. My Marilyn sits at the nexus of academia and my television screen, the crossroads where I stand unable to make that terrible decision to kill, unknowingly, the father. So this crossroads doubles into the space where I have met the sphinx of Marilyn and her suicide, a monstrous female that keeps asking me and itself, "How does it end? What does it mean?" There have been no one-line answers to this riddled identity, but I have thought about the ques-

90s.[7] Anthony Summers's 1985 *Goddess: The Secret Lives of Marilyn Monroe* alleged that Bobby Kennedy, Peter Lawford, and the FBI had been involved in a cover-up around Marilyn's death, primarily to obscure evidence of her sexual involvement with both the president and the attorney general.[8] Summers appeared on talk shows alongside other authors and investigators who claimed foul play in the circumstances surrounding Marilyn's death. In Robert Slatzer's 1992 *The Marilyn Files*, and in the television special of the same name, the Kennedys, the Mafia, and the CIA were again linked to a cover-up around Marilyn's death.[9] In Detective Milo Speriglio and Adela Gregory's 1993 *Crypt 33: The Saga of Marilyn Monroe: The Final Word*, the authors present extensive documentation of a coverup and conspiracy around Marilyn's death. This is the second time that Speriglio has told this story in book

---

tion as a way of beginning to answer it. I decided to live on the outskirts of the plague-ridden city and to talk for a while to this terrible sphinx, remembering patriarchy back at the first crossroads, the ones that led me to the gates of the city. I prefer to think of the experience as theory in exile, in a place where exile is a kind of involvement, a way of staying engaged by watching and talking from the gates—outside, but almost in. This is what I will think of as Marilyn country. Inhabiting "Marilyn country" requires a kind of productive schizophrenia, a state Norman Mailer understands quite well. For Marilyn refuses the simple dichotomies of fact and fiction, fantasy and history, as she is made up over the years, and even as she made herself up during her lifetime.

7. Norman Mailer, *Marilyn* (New York: Grosset and Dunlap, 1973).
8. Anthony Summers, *Goddess: The Secret Lives of Marilyn Monroe* (New York: Macmillan, 1985). Summers has also written a book on the JFK assassination, *Conspiracy* (New York: McGraw-Hill, 1980). JFK's assassination here immediately presages Summers's narration of a conspiracy around Marilyn's death. One conspiracy investigation leads to another.
9. Robert Slatzer, *The Marilyn Files* (New York: S.P.I. Books, 1992). The television program of the same name aired in 1992, and was produced with the help of Slatzer, who has spent years investigating the circumstances surrounding Marilyn's death. In 1974 he published *The Life and Curious Death of Marilyn Monroe* (Los Angeles: Pinnacle Books, 1974), in which he detailed alleged relations between Marilyn and the Kennedys, as well as providing political information that he believed had been recorded in Marilyn's famous, lost "red diary."

form: he also penned *The Marilyn Conspiracy* in 1986.[10] Collaborators in the project of remembering Marilyn have gone beyond her death to her afterlife. In a truly strange book published in 1992, *The Murder of Marilyn Monroe*, four "psychic" authors claim they've conducted interviews with the star from beyond the grave, and that she has named as her killers an FBI agent and two mobsters.[11] Though Marilyn was only able to die once, rememberings of her end breathe life back into the dead star, casting her in roles and histories that relate her to the "legitimate and illegitimate" bodies politic of the last several decades, including the Kennedys, Castro, and Khrushchev.

The making of these bodies politic reveals relationships to American political history, as various remembered bodies are made to constitute relationships to political orders and communities. The stories told in these rememberings are not consistent; indeed, they often contradict one another. Sometimes Marilyn is represented as the quintessential American blonde led astray by the Kennedys. In other rememberings, she has been presented as a communist spy working against the Kennedys and American democracy.[12] Marilyn assumes multiform meanings: readers encounter a woman who serves alternately as a dangerous passageway between the U.S. government and Cuban or Soviet powers, and a woman who is used as a pawn in someone else's dangerous game of politics. Considering such rememberings of Marilyn, one

10. Milo Speriglio and Adela Gregory, *Crypt 33: The Saga of Marilyn Monroe: The Final Word* (New York: Birch Lane Publishing Group, 1993).

11. Leonore Canevari, Jeanette van Wyhe, Christian Dimas, and Rachel Dimas, *The Murder of Marilyn Monroe* (New York: Carroll and Graf, 1992). All of the interviews were conducted posthumously, with the authors "contacting" JFK, Robert Kennedy, Marilyn, and a host of others who would have been difficult to assemble in the same room while alive. After death, a kind of egalitarian structure is effected and all of the famous are available for the Fresno, California, psychics to "channel" and question. The death of the author is here enacted in a curious form: dead subjects "tell their own story" through previously unknown psychics.

12. See Chapter 4 for a discussion of a *Weekly World News* article that accuses Marilyn of being a communist spy.

might posit that she enters the political only by association with other figures—figures decidedly male and associated with clear positions of political power. But such an explanation of Marilyn's role in contemporary memory would not adequately convey the political cultural condition of our time. It is not simply because she allegedly had affairs with the Kennedys that Marilyn is remembered in the 80s and 90s, but rather because she operates as a representative character who continues to be reproduced in a host of cultural channels that map the complex terrain of our political culture in late-twentieth-century America.[13]

The Nature of Representative Characters

The representative character is a cultural figure through whom the character of political life is articulated.[14] American political culture is thick with such figures, ranging from Abraham Lincoln to Frederick Douglass, from Martin Luther King, Jr., to John F. Kennedy. The representative character's life is made to chart various cultural courses. These figures convey the character of authority, legitimacy, and power in a culture through the vehicle of their lives and persons. The representative character embodies and expresses achievement, success, fail-

13. I use "America" throughout the text to refer to the United States. I choose to use the word America for its resonances as marker of a generic nation and mass-mediated political cultural condition/terrain.

14. I am influenced in this definition by Ralph Waldo Emerson's *Representative Men* (1850; reprint, Boston: Houghton Mifflin Co., 1988). I discuss this text in greater detail in Chapter 3, and in *Representative Women: Unsettling Portraits of Still Lives* (forthcoming). Emerson's representative subject is an exemplary figure through whom a cultural order is expressed. Emerson is influenced in his formulation by Plutarch. He further stresses that the representative character may operate as the vehicle of education in a democratic order. Emerson therefore engages in the process of telling stories about great men's lives, hoping to inculcate possibilities of improved character and achievement in the American citizenry. My use of the term *representative character* is not limited to the Emersonian development and use, as will become clear throughout this Introduction.

ure, genius, struggle, triumph, and other human possibilities: one representative character's story may be written as a cautionary tale, while another's may be erected as a monument to human achievement. The influence and expression of the representative characters are not limited to their immediate lifetimes: these figures become sites of recollection after their deaths. And so an ex-slave such as Frederick Douglass may be a representative character in his age and beyond, as his person and story are made to mediate values, histories, and relations social and political to generations of American citizens. The values, histories, possibilities, and identities Douglass is made to express change over time as he is remembered by various persons in different relations to slavery, African-American history and identity, issues of gender, his historical period, and in short, to America itself. This is true of all representative characters, as they exist at the intersection of cultural production and consumption, circulating in specific times and places where they are made to mediate values to a given community.

My use of the term *representative character* is related to that of Bellah et al. in *Habits of the Heart*. The authors define a representative character as:

> A kind of symbol. It is a way by which we can bring together in one concentrated image the way people in a given social environment organize and give meaning and direction to their lives. In fact, a representative character is more than a collection of individual traits and personalities. It is rather a public image that helps define, for a given group of people, just what kinds of personality traits it is good and legitimate to develop. A representative character provides an ideal, a point of reference and focus, that gives living expression to a vision of life. . . . Representative characters are not abstract ideals or faceless social roles, but are realized in the lives of those individuals who succeed more or less well in fusing their individual personalities with the public requirement of those roles.[15]

---

15. Robert N. Bellah, Richard Madsen, William M. Sullivan, Ann Swidler, and Steven M. Tipton, *Habits of the Heart: Individualism and Commitment in American Life* (New York: Harper and Row, 1985), 39.

My definition of *representative character* builds on, but is not identical to, the above definition. I understand single representative subjects to represent a multiplicity of values. Replacing "an ideal" and "a point of reference" with "a plurality of competing representative characters and discourses" would better reflect both the diversity endemic to political life and the particularities of cultural modes of representation. Further, I understand the representative character to convey to given communities both positive and negative values, visions, and histories. Finally, as the meaning of specific representative characters changes over time, particular lives may be read as more or less successful expressions of a community's values, aspirations, and achievements.

In this book I use Marilyn Monroe as a representative character through whom to approach the political cultural condition of our time. Remembered as product or story or some hybrid of the two, the representative character operates as a site on which American political culture is written and exchanged.[16] Consequently, the representative character is not simply available as shared story but also for sale as product. Particularly striking is the excessive commodification that accompanies, and is made possible through, iconographic rememberings of representative characters.[17] Once the representative character is imaged as icon, she is easily reproduced on any number of objects: hats, books, pillows, plaster busts, jewelry, calendars, clocks. Indeed, iconographic remem-

16. For a theory of the hybrid subject, see Donna J. Haraway, "The Cyborg Manifesto: Science, Technology, and Socialist-Feminism in the Late Twentieth Century," in *Simians, Cyborgs, and Women: The Reinvention of Nature* (New York: Routledge, 1991), 161–66 and 173–81.

17. Cultural remembering, as I understand it here, is not limited to narrative circulation and construction: it is also made manifest through the production of images and artifacts. These "iconographic" rememberings rely on iconic images, rather than narrativity, to communicate their subject. The icon is reproduced on an object as a means of imprinting a history, person, ideology, etc., on the surface. This image then not only communicates explicit messages and histories, it also becomes an object of memory in and of itself. For further discussion, see Chapter 2 and Roland Barthes, "Myth Today," trans. Annette Lavers, *Mythologies* (New York: Hill and Wang, 1972).

bering as a mode of circulating the representative political subject abounded in the 1980s, and continues on into the 90s.[18] Examples of this phenomenon range from the 1992 resurgence of Malcolm X as an iconic force in both popular and mass-mediated culture, to the 1980s circulation of Reagan himself.[19]

The mass media have helped to make the representative character a common means of relaying stories and constructing histories which are easily circulated and imaged across great distances of time and space. The mass-mediated representative character operates as a figure through whom multiple meanings, references, and roles are remembered. The

18. The iconographic is one of four modes of remembering that will be analyzed throughout this text. For a methodological explanation, see the last section of the Introduction.

19. Malcolm X's cultural remembering would make an excellent subject for an analysis along the lines of *American Monroe*. In fact, there has already been some dialogue concerning his "return." From December of 1992 to April of 1993, the Walker Art Center in Minneapolis featured a show on the cultural construction of Malcolm X entitled "Malcolm X: Man, Ideal, Icon." Curated by Kelli Jones, it featured paintings, sculpture, video, T-shirts, necklaces, hats, calendars, and installations examining "the legacy of the most charismatic African-American leaders of the 1960s" (brochure for show). Of particular interest was the comment book in which musuem visitors wrote their responses to the show. I particularly enjoyed the comment, "Malcolm X is history," which resonated in a number of ways, given that the show focused on both his death and his present iconic existence. For a discussion of the Walker Art Center's exhibit, see Darrell Moore, "The X Factor," *New Art Examiner*, 20, no. 8 (April 1993). A number of Malcolm X books came out the same year as the film. See David Gallen, comp., *Malcolm A to X: The Man and His Ideas* (New York: Carroll and Graf, 1992); Bernard Quina Doctor, *Malcolm X for Beginners* (New York: Writers and Readers Press, 1992); Kevin Ovendon, *Malcolm X: Socialism and Black Nationalism* (London, Chicago: Bookmarks, 1992); and Spike Lee with Ralph Wiley, *By Any Means Necessary: The Trials and Tribulations of the Making of Malcolm X* (New York: Hyperion, 1992), which includes the screenplay.

It will be interesting to see how long the X commodities remain on the market. Will X last as long as Marilyn and Elvis as commodity fetish? Or will he return to a status that is not as prevalent in popular cultural dress and product? Does he signal radical possibilities of remembering, or does he demonstrate the

pervasive presence of the mass media in contemporary daily life helps to illuminate and rapidly circulate constructions of late-twentieth-century representative character(s). The common ground for telling stories, circulating images, and reconstructing the past in the present gives ample opportunity for the construction and contestation of contemporary representative characters. Whether presidential candidates, movie stars, or both, their simulated presence in the mass media destabilizes an understanding of some "political" realm populated by those who exist apart from "culture."[20] The representative character indexes the metamorphosing body of political representation—indeed, the changing contours of the body politic itself as effected through and as the media.

By the 1980s, the mass-mediated realm of appearance had become an increasingly common means of circulating an American political cul-

---

ease with which the iconic process can level political cultural contexts and criticisms? For further discussion of X as commodity and vehicle for cultural memory, see "The X Factor," *TRANSITION: An International Review*, no. 56. Of particular interest are David Bradley, "Malcolm's Myth Making," 20–46; Michael Eric Dyson, "Martin and Malcolm," 46–59; and "Generation X: A Conversation with Spike Lee and Henry Louis Gates," 176–90.

On Reagan, see Michael Rogin, *Ronald Reagan The Movie: And Other Episodes in American Political Demonology* (Berkeley: University of California Press, 1987). For a discussion of the Washington press corps and the Reagan presidency see Mark Hertsgaard, *On Bended Knee: The Press and the Reagan Presidency* (New York: Farrar, Strauss, Giroux, 1988). Also noteworthy is Jeffrey Tulis, *The Rhetorical President* (Princeton, N.J.: Princeton University Press, 1987). Rogin's Reagan also appears in Chapter 1.

20. I am working from such a model by not divorcing the "cultural" from the "political." I begin with an understanding of subjects who inhabit both realms simultaneously. This model does not exclude traditional or formal understandings of political practices such as voting, for example. It seeks, rather, to remember the cultural location and locution of voting politics and practices. How were the voting citizens represented at a given moment in campaign literature? How did a disenfranchised group seek to represent itself in relation to the dominant class? What sorts of inclusions and exclusions followed from the political cultural representation of this voting subject? How did the ways in which a disenfranchised group employed terms from the dominant political discourse transform the very terms of representation? Political cultural under-

tural "center."[21] As the media saturate, constitute, and mirror daily life, they comprise a common ground of images, stories, events, and information that form a base of cultural belonging. The political "center" could now be read as an operant term for the common ground circulated and mediated through the channels of a mass communications matrix. This realm evades models of "center" that posit both a margin and a middle: the center is central by being everywhere and nowhere all at once.[22] Dispersed over time and space, encountered and traversed on television screens and tabloid racks, this center functions as a space where people, issues, and events may "appear" before the culture at large.

---

standings of representation are thus multivalent. Who is representing a subject; how they are representing that subject; ways in which the subject is not being represented; the terms of representation themselves—all of these inform a political cultural understanding of representation.

21. This is a variation of Hannah Arendt's "space of appearance," which I discuss further in Chapter 1. In The Human Condition (Chicago: University of Chicago Press, 1958), Arendt writes: "The polis . . . is the organization of the people as it arises out of acting and speaking together, and its true space lies between people living together for this purpose, wherever they happen to be. . . . [I]t is the space of appearance in the widest sense of the word, namely, the space where I appear to others as others appear to me. . . . [T]his space does not always exist. . . . [N]o man, moreover, can live in it all the time" 198–99. I wish to transform Arendt's description of space. As simulation explodes the possibilities of appearance, the site of "the space of appearance" opens up. Yet virtual spaces of appearance do not necessarily express the agency and possibility for communication that Arendt assigns to the space of appearance. In this altered phenomological state, the present text might be read as a meditation on the ontological and epistemological possibilities and limitations of democratic praxis in the simulated terrains of postmodern nation-states.

22. It also resists the exclusionary tactics of privileging and privileged knowledges, as discussed in Michel Foucault, "Foucault Responds to Sartre," in John Johnston, trans., Sylvere Lotringer, ed. Foucault Live (New York: Semiotext(e) Foreign Agents Series, 1989). According to Foucault:

Today more than ever the transmission of knowledge (savoir) is extensive and efficacious. . . . Knowledge was once a secret, and the authenticity of knowledge was at the same time protected by the fact that this knowledge didn't circulate or circulated only among a strictly defined number of people; as soon as knowl-

Mass-mediated culture is characterized by its relationship to accelerated circulation. This circulation is reliant on both technologies of production/dissemination — television, film, radio, newspapers, mass-fiction, etc.—and mediators of culture—those who buy, watch, listen, and read cultural products. A form of remembering occurs as the cultural mediator encounters the mass-circulated story, product, image, and so on. The mediator may respond to the circulation in a number of ways. She may read it. She may ignore it. She may register it. She may interpret it, and thereby rewrite it. I do not seek to measure the various ways in which cultural mediators have remembered Marilyn in such "popular" rememberings. My goal is rather to interpret and genealogically track some of the ways of being and knowing expressed through mass-mediated rememberings of Marilyn Monroe. Certainly, various interpretations and appropriations of these rememberings could transform their meanings. I am studying, however, the mass-mediated modes of ordering power and knowledge in these rememberings, regardless of potential popular intervention and transformation.[23]

<hr>

edge was made public, it ceased to be knowledge and consequently ceased to be true.

Today we are at a very developed stage of a mutation that began in the 17th and 18th centuries when knowledge became a kind of public thing. To know was to see clearly what every individual placed in the same conditions could see and verify. To that extent the structure of knowledge became public. . . . [T]here weren't ignorant people on one side and scholars on the other. What happened at one point in knowledge is very quickly reflected at another point. . . . [N]ever has it communicated with itself more quickly (43).

23. Certainly, it can be said of any text that various interventions on the part of the reader/mediator will affect the force of dominant codes. We may change the "meaning" of a text by playing with it, placing various restraints on it, imagining someone other than the protagonist in the position of the protagonist, and so on. It is not my point to claim that any text is beyond these sorts of interventions. I want to stress at the same time, however, that the readings I am conducting are looking at the sorts of cultural logics operant in the various rememberings of Marilyn without then imagining a variety of rereadings, or openings, of these texts.

This project does not place mass-mediated rememberings fully in the realm of popular culture. To flesh out the form of this project, it is useful to spend a moment contrasting my model of mass-mediated culture with John Fiske's understanding of popular culture. Fiske maintains that popular culture arises as "the people" respond to the dominant culture: "Popular culture is made . . . out of the resources, both discursive and material, that are provided by the social system that disempowers."[24]

He proceeds to argue that the "resources" employed by the people in the construction of popular culture continue to "carry the interests of the economically and ideologically dominant." For this reason, Fiske argues that popular culture is "contradictory and conflictual to the core." Hence, "popular culture is always in process," and its meanings must therefore be read intertextually by taking into account social and historical relations. Context, then, is crucial in the formation of a popular culture that Fiske describes in terms of resistance: its renegade quality is made possible and legible against the backdrop of a dominant order.

Fiske's theories of popular culture seek to articulate the ways in which "the subordinate" work to control their lives through semiotic fields of resistance. He writes: "The basic power of the dominant in capitalism may be economic, but this economic power is both underpinned and exceeded by semiotic power, that is, the power to make meanings. So semiotic resistance that not only refuses the dominant meanings but constructs opposite ones that serve the interests of the subordinate is as vital a base for the redistribution of power as is evasion. The ability to think differently, to construct one's own meanings of self and of social relations, is the necessary ground without which no political action can hope to succeed."[25]

What occurs in the production and reproduction of popular culture according to this model is a political-semiotic balancing act played out through a series of actions and reactions between the micro and macro realms of political culture. Fiske's model of semiotic resistance points to

24. John Fiske, *Understanding Popular Culture* (Boston: Unwin Hyman, 1989), 3.
25. Ibid., 9.

the politically subversive strategies operant in reading, viewing, listening, and making practices. These strategies transform "dominant" cultural meanings through rewritings of seemingly "fixed" products/spaces/ productions.

Fiske is optimistic about popular culture's potential to empower the possibilities of power. He chooses a model of popular culture over a notion of mass culture, a category that makes no sense to him. He sees "mass culture" as a contradiction in terms, since "the people" do not behave as "a mass."[26] Fiske stresses that "a homogeneous, externally produced culture cannot be sold ready-made to the masses: culture simply does not work like that."[27] To deem those who interact with mass culture as "the masses" is to position them generally as nameless, faceless, and powerless.[28] Though I agree with Fiske that "mass culture" is itself oxymoronic, I further posit that there is such a thing as mass-mediated culture. Mass-mediated culture comprises the images, stories, persons— in short, the host of productions—circulated through the mass media. In order for a product or event to exist in mass-mediated culture, it must

26. Fiske defines the people this way in *Understanding Popular Culture*: "'The people' is not a stable sociological category; it cannot be identified and subjected to empirical study, for it does not exist in objective reality. The people, the popular, the popular forces, are a shifting set of allegiances that cross all social categories; various individuals belong to different popular formations at different times, often moving between them quite fluidly. By 'the people,' then, I mean the shifting set of social allegiances, which are described better in terms of people's felt collectivity than in terms of external sociological factors such as class, gender, age, race, region, or what have you" (24).

27. Ibid., 10–11.

28. A notable refutation of this account is Jean Baudrillard's characterization of the masses in *In the Shadow of the Silent Majorities,* trans. Paul Foss, John Johnston, and Paul Patton (New York: Semiotext(e) Foreign Agent Series, 1983), and discussed at greater length in Chapter 4. Baudrillard considers the masses, or the silent majority, to be empowered precisely by their dislocation and "apparent" apathy: "Let us not make them [the masses] into a new and glorious reference. For one thing, they do not exist. But note that all power flounders on this silent majority, which is neither an entity nor a sociological reality, but the shadow cast by power, its sinking vortex, its form of absorption" (48).

be widely circulated through mass channels. Mass-mediated remember-ings are not dependent on "the people"; they also reverberate and re-produce within the mass communications matrix, where they take on a life of their own above and apart from popular culture.[29] Cultural me-diators may interpret and make their own meanings from cultural productions as they engage in a Fiskean model of popular cultural pro-duction, but they may also simply act as the sociocultural membranes through which mass-mediated messages pass.

Mass-mediated rememberings authorize public being while simulta-neously eroding older forms of popular representation. The mass media may well be a democratizing force, but the form of democracy they con-stitute transforms older notions of liberty, equality, and justice for all. The "right to representation," once a revolutionary insistence in the ar-ticulation of an American self, has been translated under conditions of normative mass mediation into the "right to be *as* representation." Mass-mediated rememberings and representations image public being and political cultural "reality."[30] The circulation of an issue or figure through mass-mediated channels serves to grant a form of "real" public status.[31] A public space is created by virtue of appearance in the mass-

29. "Matrix" denotes the dynamic generative character of mass communications systems. It is a series of points through which meaning is delivered via mass mediation. At the same time, it constitutes a cultural aporia through which the graphie that register cultural consciousness may be read. This is not to say that any one product reproduces the culture in toto; rather, the culture mutates and resonates through the interstices of the matrix. For further discussion of the matrix as a gendered term indexing the media as womb and site of reproduc-tion, see Chapter 2.

30. For an engaging analysis of "reality" and public being, see Marilyn Frye, "To Be and Be Seen: The Politics of Reality," in *The Politics of Reality: Essays in Feminist Theory* (Freedom, Wisc.: The Crossing Press Feminist Series, 1983).

31. The coverage of sexual harassment as both sociocultural reality and media issue during and after the Anita Hill/Clarence Thomas hearings stands as a particularly salient illustration of the relationship between mediation and le-gitimation. As Anita Hill became a mass-mediated representative character il-luminating issues of sexual harassment, the issue itself was addressed with greater frequency throughout the mass communications matrix. The Senate

mediated realm, in a democracy that may or may not have citizens. The citizens of the mass-mediated body politic inhabit a collective virtual terrain, as they are remembered into a virtual community of memory.

Political cultural rememberings posit terms of identity, history, and community through their circulation. "Re-membering" as I understand it here is a material process between persons and texts, replacing the citizen/mediator into the political cultural body politic. I hyphenate "re-membering" to emphasize its force as literal and figurative form of cultural "re-collection." The literal role of remembering is evidenced as an incorporation of the mediator/citizen into the codes and orders of the greater political cultural economy through her relation to a common repository of memory. The citizen is made a member of the body politic by participating in its shared language and legacy—by being "re-membered" into collective life. The figurative role of re-membering is enacted through the circulation of images and stories in the political cultural economy. Events, persons, characters, bodies, accounts, etc., are thus re-collected and redistributed in and through the varied sites of re-membering.

Political cultural remembering is neither a static nor a stereotypic process. Cultures rely on differing modes of remembering in relation to differences in technologies, discursive practices, gender relations and roles, relations between public and private realms, the place of the citi-

---

Judiciary Committee hearings took place in the mass-mediated realm of appearance, under the camera's watching eye. One mass-mediated channel gave way to another: after the hearings, *People* and *Time* both devoted cover stories to "the issue" of sexual harassment. And these mainstream magazines were not singular in this action, nor did the coverage and equation come to an end in the weeks following the hearing. From conservative journals to women's magazines, Anita Hill and the issue of sexual harassment were transmitted as one and the same. The public's attention is now drawn to "the reality of sexual harassment," as sexual harassment appears as a more widely acknowledged aspect of "reality." Once represented and remembered in the public mass-mediated economy, the issue was charged with a greater degree of "presence" and authority.

zen in the body politic, and so on. In contemporary American society, rememberings operate in the realm of appearance *in medias res*.[32] The mechanisms of these rememberings inform subjects in a panoply of media seldom based on "live" experience. Technologically reproduced, these mass-mediated rememberings insert the citizen into a virtual collective space often entered alone. In this virtual realm of appearance, discursive acts and figures serve as the material of the "real." In mass-mediated culture, remembering and re-membering occur simultaneously: the literal and figurative roles of memory are conflated. From CNN coverage of the Gulf War to *People* magazine meditations on Camelot, mass-mediated rememberings situate the cultural mediator in relation to an event or historical era through the membrane of the media. We encounter America through the vehicle of the media as we too are remembered into history, through the locus of the image. We know who we are and where we have been by how we are remembered *in medias res*.

Mass-mediated rememberings relay technologies of power and knowledge. They are conversations about the representative forms and characters of political culture. The ways in which we as members of a culture are able to use knowledge also reflect and inform the ways in which we may exercise power. What we claim to know shapes the people we can and want to be. Studying power, then, means studying forms of knowledge.[33] I am studying the forms of power and knowledge relayed through mass-mediated rememberings of the representative character Marilyn Monroe. *American Monroe* is a political cultural grammar to accompany mass-mediated rememberings of Marilyn's body politic.

32. I define and discuss "*in medias res*" in greater detail in Chapter 1.
33. I am particularly influenced in this approach by Michel Foucault. See particularly the discussion of power and knowledge in "Two Lectures," in Colin Gordon, ed., *Power/Knowledge: Selected Interviews and Other Writings 1972–1977* (New York: Pantheon, 1980), 78–108. See particularly page 93, where he states, "There can be no possible exercise of power without a certain economy of discourses of truth which operates through and on the basis of this association. We are subjected to the production of truth through power and we cannot ex-

Why Marilyn?

Constructions of Marilyn Monroe allow for a much more developed examination of mass-mediated remembering than would be possible with a
lesser-known figure. While one could engage in similar interpretations of
other figures (Michael Jackson or Madonna) or other events (the filmic
representation of the Vietnam War), I find Marilyn to be especially useful
for several reasons. These include her status as an icon of femininity (both
as female body and as sign for "woman"), her chronological relationship
to the 1960s, her association with the Kennedys, her "Americanness" and
that of her biographers, her relationship to simulation and the mass media, her status as mythico-religious figure, and the character of her problematic death. These characteristics mark Marilyn as a body on which
contestations over gender, the political character of culture, processes of
simulation in contemporary America, current regimes of knowledge and
power, and the forms of mass-mediated historical consciousness have
been and continue to be written.

Marilyn ironically embodies the postmodern character of late-twentieth-century American political culture.[34] This character is made up of
forms that straddle "high" and "low" culture and collapse discrete divisions of time and space. Postmodernism signals the dissolution of fixed

---

ercise power except through the production of truth." For power, knowledge,
and the study of discourse, see "Politics and the Study of Discourse" and
"Governmentality" in Graham Burchell, Colin Gordon, and Peter Miller,
eds., *The Foucault Effect* (London: Harvester, 1991).

34. For a lucid and engaging definition of "postmodernism," see Todd Gitlin,
"Postmodernism Defined at Last," *Utne Reader*, July/August 1989, 52–61.
Michael Shapiro has also written a provocative and convincing defense of post-
modernism in his *Reading the Postmodern Polity: Political Theory as Textual
Practice* (Minneapolis: University of Minnesota Press, 1992). Shapiro argues
for a political theory capable of addressing the various sites of political culture
in the late twentieth century, including film, novels, theme parks, and so on.
For a discussion of postmodernism's various forms, see Frederic Jameson,
Postmodernism, or the Cultural Logic of Late Capitalism (Durham, N.C.: Duke
University Press, 1991). See also Michael Ryan, *Working Hypotheses for a Post-
Revolutionary Society* (Baltimore, Md.: The Johns Hopkins Press, 1989), esp.

identities and the advent of unholy marriages. Schizophrenic combina-
tions of fashions, forms, categories, identities, genres, bodies, persons,
nations, and ethnicities are the norm under postmodernism.[35] The
same may be said of Marilyn's body, character, and identity in contemporary culture: she is never fully situated in any one time or place, but
rather is reproduced and disseminated ad infinitum as towel, food item,
book, photograph, 1950s starlet, 1990s corpse, ashtray, Madonna, calendar girl, greeting card, etc.[36] Though she once expressed the body of a

---

ch. 4, and Andrew Ross, ed., *Universal Abandon: The Politics of Postmodernism*
(Minneapolis: University of Minnesota Press, 1988).

 I am in particular agreement with Gianni Vattimo's definition of postmodernity and his emphasis on mass media in *The Transparent Society*, trans.
David Webb (Baltimore, Md.: The Johns Hopkins Press, 1992). He writes:

 "Much is said about postmodernity nowadays. So much, in fact, that it has
become almost obligatory to distance oneself from the notion, to see it as a fad
and to insist on its having been overcome. It is my belief, however, that the
term 'postmodern' has a meaning, and that this meaning is linked to the fact
that the society in which we live is a society of generalized communication. It
is the society of the mass media" (1).

35. See Gilles Deleuze and Félix Guattari, *Anti-Oedipus: Capitalism and Schizophrenia,* trans. Robert Hurley, Mark Seem, and Helen R. Lane (Minneapolis:
University of Minnesota Press, 1983), esp. 240–62.

36. The above is only a partial list of Marilyn's cultural incarnations. Though
Marilyn's name and image are licensed by the Roger Richman agency in Beverly Hills, she is often reproduced without permission and appears in an almost
endless variety of sites. From popular murals on Hollywood Boulevard to
Andy Warhol's 1964 Marilyn diptych, to collector's plates and special issues of
magazines such as the February 1988 *L.A. Style* entitled "Marilyn: Lost Images,"
the range of these reproductions blurs the boundaries between the corporate
and kitsch, the popular and the mass-mediated, the highbrow and the lowbrow.
Photographers such as Bert Stern have written biographies around her photographs; see Bert Stern with Annie Gottlieb, *The Last Sitting* (New York:
William Morrow and Company, 1982), and *Marilyn Among Friends,* written by
two of Marilyn's friends, Sam Shaw and Norman Rosten (New York: Henry
Holt and Company, 1987). And in a particularly striking reproduction of Marilyn, John Rechy's *Marilyn's Daughter* (New York: Carroll and Graf, 1988)
imagines the travels and travails of "Normalyn," love child and living testament
to Marilyn's alleged affair with Robert F. Kennedy. I discuss these and other
"graphic" rememberings of Marilyn in subsequent chapters.

"1950s America," and may still represent nostalgia for that era, she is no longer confined to this referent because she has moved out of the "50s" by translating into simulation.[37] Indeed, she signals both presence and loss as her body/image must also always signify her death—the removal of her body from the living world and its resurrection in the virtual spaces of mass mediation by means of simulation and mechanical reproduction. Finally, the unanswered question of her suicide further riddles her representative forms with excess possibilities of conspiracy, controversy, and cover-up.

Contestations abound in rememberings of Marilyn. She is remembered as victim, heroine, queen bitch, unattainable sex object, frigid sex symbol, dumb blonde, feminist, communist, political pawn, communist spy, photographic object, biographical subject, material object, material girl, and media manipulator. She is a surface on which different bodies, identities, and histories may be reconstructed. In *Pornography and Silence*, feminist Susan Griffin interprets "graphic" representations of Marilyn as characteristic of the violence directed at the female subject under what she deems a patriarchal and pornographic cultural order.[38]

37. In *Postmodernism*, Jameson refers to a 1959 Philip K. Dick novel, *Time Out of Joint*, in which the fifties are evoked by: "President Eisenhower's stroke; Main Street, U.S.A.; Marilyn Monroe; a world of neighbors and PTAs; small retail chain stores; favorite television programs," etc. (283). Yet even in Dick's novel this 1950s world turns out to be a simulation constructed in 1997, "in the midst of an interstellar atomic civil war," as a means of tricking the protagonist into working as a government agent. In this novel, written while Marilyn was still alive, she is already both a sign of the 1950s and of the future: an icon who shatters models of the historical that seek to cement historical period and referent. For further discussion, see Jameson, *Postmodernism*, 279–88, and Philip K. Dick, *Time Out of Joint* (1959; reprint, New York: Vintage, 1992).

38. Susan Griffin, *Pornography and Silence: Culture's Revenge Against Nature* (New York: Harper Colophon Books, 1981). See the discussion on Marilyn Monroe on pages 6 and 204–17. Griffin takes Marilyn's exposure in life and death as paradigmatic representations of women's relationship to the pornographic consciousness. She writes, "Here is the essential tragedy of Marilyn Monroe. We sense that because she wished to reclaim her own eros, she was moved to impersonate a pornographic image of female sexuality" (214). She

Griffin uses Marilyn as both a site for remembering injustices against women and as a point of departure for overcoming an order that she believes is predicated on misogyny. Though Griffin sees Marilyn as having been victimized in many ways by Western culture's pornographic consciousness, she recalls Marilyn's story in order to expose and challenge that tradition: "We have ample evidence that whatever else she was, she was a rebel against society's sexual double standard. She would not wear bras and girdles. She refused to be ashamed of having posed in the nude."[39]

While representing the undoing of a cultural pornographic desire for Griffin, Marilyn remains the object of that desire for many others. In books ranging from H. J. Lembourn's *Diary of a Lover of Marilyn Monroe* to Bert Stern's *The Last Sitting*, Marilyn is portrayed as the object of her authors' desire, and the subject representative of American sexuality.[40] As Marilyn is explored by her male authors, they perform a "pornographic" remembering of the subject. These authors and their readers do not enter Marilyn's textual body via a critique of pornographic scripting, but rather as the site of a shared or mass-mediated desire. The act of photographing and viewing photographed subjects in this mode of remembering is meant to incite desire on the part of the reader. Stern relates his feelings photographing Marilyn: "That *energy of observing* is

---

adds, "[H]idden beneath every pornographic image of female glamour is the conviction that a woman does not really exist" (214). By repeatedly conflating "all women" and "Marilyn Monroe," Griffin uses Marilyn as the focus for her vision of the pornographic character of Western culture. She proceeds to interpret biographies, films, photographs, and other "graphic" rememberings of Marilyn to make broad generalizations such as this: "Therefore, like Marilyn Monroe, all women within this culture find ourselves caught between the Scylla and Charibdis of ordinariness and extraordinariness" (215).

39. Ibid., 212–13.
40. Hans J. Lembourn, *Diary of a Lover of Marilyn Monroe* (New York: Arbor House, 1977), and Stern, *Last Sitting*. Lembourn's account takes the form of a confessional narrative in which he confides to the reader his alleged various trysts, fights, conversations, and travels with his subject.

marvelous. When you desire someone so much, and she's right there in front of you, and there's something very special about *not* touching, and just letting *the light* caress her. And the camera plays a very powerful role in all this. . . . Since I was thirteen, I had dreamed of a woman who would roll on a bed with me and do everything I wanted. Now I had found that woman. She was vulnerable and drunk and tender and inviting and exciting. But I had a camera in my hands and a drug in my veins" (emphasis in original).[41] The woman who challenged cultural norms and conventions for Griffin is the incarnation of masculine desires and fantasies for Stern. Marilyn consists of multiform meanings.

Though the content of her representative character may change, there remains one constant: Marilyn mediates the very content and form of representation itself. Her mass-mediated relation to life as simulation and simulation as life renders her a figure always already an artifice or construct, that is, a self-referential representation. The "real Marilyn" is an oxymoron: she *mediates the real* by being a simulation of herself. In *American Monroe*, I analyze some of the "real Marilyns" that have appeared in the decades following her death. I organize the readings of these constructions through four modes of remembering: the iconographic, the biographic, the cartographic, and the hagiographic.[42] These graphia function as the means for the production and dissemination of cultural knowledges, subjects, and power. They manage and articulate the human condition at a given historical moment.

41. Stern, *Last Sitting*, 136. The above passage is not unique as a representation of Stern's description of the photographic process. He sums it up on page 162: "My love affair with Marilyn was photographic." This nexus of the pornographic and the photographic articulate Stern's desire to capture his subject.
42. In this organization of "graphia," I am drawing generally from Jacques Derrida's excursions on writing in *Of Grammatology*, trans. Gayatri Chakravorty Spivak (Baltimore, Md.: The Johns Hopkins Press, 1974). Though mass-mediated modes of remembering are related to historiography, they are not limited to it as traditional and formal historical "writing" practice. See Chapter 1, n. 1, for more on the production of history and the historical.

By focusing on the possible civic grammars that these graphia posit as cultural literacies, I wish to make explicit the assumptions—or underlying strategies and meanings—of these modes of remembering in mass-mediated culture.

In the first chapter, *In Medias Res*, I discuss political cultural rememberings of "the real" in the mass-mediated realm. I argue that the normalization of mass-mediated channels of communication has displaced the traditional division between the historical (or elite memory) and the unhistorical (or popular memory), and that current mass-mediated rememberings operate somewhere in the interstices of the two. I discuss the political stakes of claiming a "re-collected" common ground and conclude that contemporary American citizens dwell *in medias res*, inhabiting a political cultural landscape comprising representational and representative characters, figures, and languages, and participating in a community organized around the forces and forms of simulation as world-making. I stress the importance of the various "languages of belonging" endemic to the mass-mediated political landscape, and propose to examine four of these languages or modes in the chapters that follow.[43]

In the second chapter, *Ecce Signum,* I focus on the circulation and translation of icons in mass-mediated political cultural economies. I hold that the mass media promote an iconographic consciousness that relies on units and unities of story and character made available for accelerated dissemination. I examine ways in which Marilyn as icon has been associated with mechanical reproduction. I read Andy Warhol's constructions of Marilyn as an expression of the relations between commodification, the image, fame, and culture. I further contrast iconographic rememberings of Marilyn with reconstructions of the Virgin Mary, drawing on the work of theorist Margaret Miles. I question the degree to which the resurrection of this fleshy icon signals possibilities of political cultural redemption or death.

---

43. I take the term *languages of belonging* from Michael Ignatieff, *The Needs of Strangers* (New York: Viking Press, 1984).

In the third chapter, *Vita Feminae,* I contend that the biographical subject is particularly suited to modes of mass-mediated remembering in contemporary American political culture. Marilyn's biography begins in her life as she participates in the writing and rewriting of her genealogical history, life story, and original name. This project is continued after her death by her various biographers, who use Marilyn's life as an occasion to write new and old versions of American identity and history. I examine biographies of Marilyn written by two representative characters in their own right—Norman Mailer and Gloria Steinem—as they reflect the impulse to inscribe American identity on and through the figure of Marilyn, and thus, the body of woman. I analyze in particular the extent to which Steinem's revisionings of the personal as political ultimately replicate traditional notions of public selfhood, and the manner in which Mailer's relationship to mythic simulation effects a production of "the real" that confuses production and reproduction in his authoring of Marilyn.

In the fourth chapter, *Amor Fatality,* I discuss Marilyn's relationship to conspiracy and conspiracy theories. Plot and narrative come together in the cartographic mode of mapping history; the telling of Marilyn's life as conspiracy seeks to produce a series of seamless conclusions that strain to encapsulate her agency as a corruptive threat to the body politic. I pose and respond to a series of questions regarding Marilyn's emplotment in the cartographic mode. How do conspiracy theories negotiate and employ mass-mediated modes of historical remembering? How do emplotted models of historical action effect understandings of agency? To what extent do the normalized forces of the mass media effect cartographic emplotments of the historical? Why do rewritings of Marilyn as pawn or agent of contamination in conspiracies involving the Kennedys and Khrushchev emerge in 1980s America? How does the body of Marilyn figure into these conspiracy theories?

In the final chapter, *Corpus Mysticum,* I analyze Marilyn's status as corpse and suicide/problematic death. Marilyn's suicide opened up a narrative space through which her story has been continuously retold. I discuss best-selling efforts to rewrite Marilyn's end, focusing particularly on *Coroner* by "coroner to the stars" Thomas Noguchi and *Goddess* by investigative journalist Anthony Summers.[44] I see the very open-endedness of Marilyn's death as representative of a political cultural crisis. This crisis is aggravated as the suicide of any beloved figure must be aggravated: Why did this woman who "had everything" in our culture choose to kill herself? This question opens a cultural wound that is attended by the presence of Marilyn as corpse expressive of a dangerous agency. I argue that attempts to remember her death strive to bury her once and for all, even while they reopen the issue of her death. I suggest that perhaps in the postmortem condition it is neither just the author nor the subject who is dead, but the story itself. With the death of the story, however, is resurrected the simulated form, that which is simultaneously with and without bodily organs, with and without conventional political cultural presence—the mass-mediated representative character. Disseminated through mass mediation, this postmodern production of the human subject both displays and displaces older regimes of knowledge and power through its dangerously hybridized form. I conclude my discussion of the hagiographic remembering of Marilyn with her resurrection as transgressive goddess of mass-mediated culture.

44. Thomas Noguchi with Joseph DiMona, *Coroner* (New York: Simon and Schuster, 1983); Summers, *Goddess.*

Marilyn in The Seven Year Itch.
Photo by UPI/Bettman.

The emergence of the later phase of the modern nation, from the mid-nineteenth century, is also one of the most sustained periods of mass migration within the west, and colonial expansion in the east. The nation fills the void left in the uprooting of communities and kin, and turns that loss into the language of metaphor. Metaphor, as the etymology of the word suggests, transfers the meaning of home and belonging, across the "middle passage," or the central European steppes, across those distances, and cultural differences, that span the imagined community of the nation-people.

Homi Bhabha, *Nation and Narration*

A part of our definition is our common ground, and a part of it is sharing and mutually enjoying our common ground. Undoubtedly, since we are humans, a part of our definition is a recurring contest over the common ground: Who shall describe its boundaries, occupy it, use it, or own it? . . .

The danger of the phrase "common ground" is that it is likely to be meant as no more than a metaphor. I am not using it as a metaphor; I mean by it the actual ground that is shared by whatever group we may be talking about—the human race, a nation, a community, or a household.

Wendell Berry, *Home Economics*

1   In Medias Res

Marilyn Monroe lives *in medias res*. Here she is the stuff of memory, yet she also expresses the dynamic possibilities of cultural presence as simulated immortality—even the dead can live forever *in medias res*. In process, in the middle, in the matrix, the media make a virtual world where the dead and living meet. In the warm matrix of the media Marilyn comes to life. The media make her live: she is the goddess in the machine, of the machine, as the machine. But "machine" seems an archaic word for the country *in medias res* and the body of its young, dead goddess. Machines are old and cumbersome and slow, while the matrix of the mass-mediated world is young and light and fast. Indeed, this matrix moves so swiftly it seems invisible, with things disappearing into it and as magically reappearing. Newspapers, movies, magazines, pulp fiction, coffee-table clutter, computer networks, trading cards,

call-in talk shows: this world of rapidly moving pictures creates the possibility of being everywhere and nowhere all at once. The democracy of
this state is unsettling. All the people and stories and drawings and logos
and theme songs and jingles and histories collapse into each other.
Distinctions between public and private, politics and culture, female
and male, power and knowledge, past and future are lost in a euphoric
present. *In medias res.*

And this is where Marilyn lives. Her life is over, but her story has not
finished; in fact, it has flourished. She appears to citizens of the late
twentieth century as both chronologically frozen and historically fluid;
she is forever the young woman she was at the time of her death, and
yet she constantly yields to new reconstructions of her form. Her story
continues to grow, and as it grows it assumes new meanings and possibilities. Those who tell Marilyn's tale negotiate myriad ways of being in
America past and present. The dreams, conspiracy theories, photos,
tributes, postcards, and refrigerator magnets run together with increasing speed only to crash in a heap of detritus at the feet of the angel of
history. Looking back over her shoulder, Marilyn rushes forward, compelled by the wreckage piling up in her wake. Watching *her,* we get to
look into the past and the future at once, while that temporal distinction we call the present makes less and less sense as a uniform site of location. Teleologies are undone as past, present, and future are rewired
into a circulated common ground of mass-mediated memory. The matrix of the media is not linear, nor is its history. It is a web, a tangle of
wires and circuits and connections made or not made. It surrounds us
at the end of the century, remembering us *in medias res.* Bodies, narratives, landscapes, architectures, icons, events, and histories are caught
up in the network of a virtual America even as they are made to reproduce the shifting common ground(s) of our presence/present. Contestations over their meaning and place form the contours of our cultural remembering.

Paradoxically, this dynamic process of cultural remembering binds us
together even as it brings the past into the present. Virtual America is
made up of a series of competing conversations about the texture of the

real—daily life itself—in our time. Remembering does not fix the object of memory outside of the lived world; rather, it makes that object a part of the common ground on which the present may be articulated, known, and understood. Marilyn is a wonderful subject for American cultural memory. Her many contradictory qualities and histories allow for competing creations of the "real" Marilyn Monroe. And remembering is about creating what is real; it is about finding stories to tell ourselves about the past and the present. These stories help us to think about where we have been, and in the process they help us to know who we are. For this reason, memory is crucial to the formation of community. When members of a community, whether a neighborhood or a nation-state, lose their common objects of memory, they have difficulty maintaining a common ground—a *present*—on which to construct foundations of mutuality, belonging, language, and knowledge. Common memories allow a political culture to understand its past, and to imagine its future. And representative characters like Marilyn are crucial to these processes because they allow for the development of a discourse in which community is realized, belonging becomes a possibility, and knowledge is circulated throughout the political culture. Yet these rememberings are always shifting, as is the ground of the virtual network of mass-mediated culture. And so, as we traffic in the wreckage of the real, we may focus on particular representative characters who have been made to express competing constructions of the virtual community at a given moment.

But what sort of common ground of memory is realized in our culture's diverse constructions of Marilyn Monroe? Marilyn Monroe is a representative character that expresses the reconstituted body politic of late-twentieth-century America. Marilyn was not a president, she was an actress who may have slept with a president; still, she has much to teach us about relations between power and knowledge, the public and the private, and gender and language in our time. In the cultural imagination, she embodies positions of power and powerlessness; she presides as both the exceptional figure and the working-class Norma Jean. Rememberings of Marilyn occur in the interstices of the "historical" and the "unhistorical," the "political" and the "personal."[1] From the White House to the Kremlin, she inhabits spaces where her linkage with other representative characters mirrors the reconstitution of the body politic; even the brothers Kennedy are remembered through her form, and on her terms. In this way, Marilyn corresponds to the postmodern body politic: she is in no one place but is rather the occupant and expression of a virtual America circulated through the mass media.

Rememberings of Marilyn express an irresolvable tension between the longing for a unitary and stable subject and the impossibilities of the same. The insistence on the reality of the different versions of Marilyn's cultural incarnations results in a sort of political cultural schizophrenia: hosts of "real, final, and true" Marilyns are reproduced in various media,

---

1. Mass-mediated rememberings confuse the "historical" and the "unhistorical." Characterizations of history writ large do not always encompass the "micropro-ductions" of daily political cultural life. In *The Content of the Form* (Baltimore, Md.: The Johns Hopkins Press, 1987), Hayden White contends that:

> All theoretical discussions of historiography become enmeshed in the ambiguity contained in the notion of history itself. . . . This ambiguity derives, not from the fact that the term history refers both to an object of study and to an account of this object, but from the fact that the object of study itself can be conceived only on the basis of an equivocation. I refer, of course, to the equivocation contained in the notion of a general human past that is split into two parts one of which is supposed to be "historical," and the other, "unhistorical.". . . For this is to sug-gest that there are two orders of humanity, one of which is more human—be-cause it is more historical—than the other (55).

The "historical" here is associated with those occupying institutionally recog-nized positions of authority, as well as those who challenge or otherwise influ-ence the construction of such centralized power. The "unhistorical" is aligned with popular culture—the memories, traditions, and activities associated with the "common" people, expressed in non-formalized discourses. These remem-berings center on "small" events and persons, on the activities and practices of daily life, on regional, filial, and biographical histories. These popular produc-tions are not generally understood in relation to history writ large as having an effect on global political cultural orders, but rather are meaningful in relation to local communities of memory.

each version claiming to most realistically re(as)semble the star.[2] Ironically, this cultural schizophrenia resonates with Marilyn's genealogical legacy: her mother was diagnosed as a paranoid schizophrenic, as was her grandmother, and she herself suffered mental illnesses throughout her life.[3] Now Marilyn's "presence" in American mass-mediated society expresses the breakdown of temporality and unitary identity, as the dizzying excess of her production signals the "euphoria" that Fredric Jameson associates with the experience of postmodernism.[4] To Jameson, the "cultural logic of late capitalism" promotes a form of political cultural schizophrenia that levels time and place into the experience of space, thereby producing a "breakdown of the signifying chain . . . [which results in] a series of pure and unrelated presents."[5] According to Jameson, "The great Warhol figures—Marilyn herself, or Edie Sedgwick—the notorious burn-out cases of the 1960s, and the great dominant experiences of drugs and schizophrenia—these would seem to have little enough in common anymore, either with the hysterics and neurotics of Freud's own day, or with those canonical experiences of radical isolation and solitude, anomie, private revolt, Van Gogh–type madness, which dominated the period of high modernism. This shift in cultural pathology can be characterized as one in which the alienation of the subject is displaced by the fragmentation of the subject."[6]

2. For an extensive analysis of mechanical reproduction and schizophrenia, see Gilles Deleuze and Félix Guattari, *Anti-Oedipus: Capitalism and Schizophrenia,* trans. Robert Hurley, Mark Seem, and Helen R. Cane (Minneapolis: University of Minnesota Press, 1983), 34.

3. For an extended discussion of this subject, see Lucy Freeman, *Why Norma Jean Killed Marilyn Monroe: A Psychological Portrait* (Mamaroneck, N.Y.: Hastings House, 1992).

4. Fredric Jameson, "Postmodernism, or the Cultural Logic of Late Capitalism," *New Left Review* 146 (1984): 73.

5. Ibid., 71.

6. Ibid., 63.

The matrix of the media gives birth to the fragmented subject. This subject is not alienated because it has no one original location. It has no single history, no point of origin, no final end: it lives as copy, resurrected as image through the forces of mass-mediated reproduction. The fragmented subject exists through the traffic of representation, realized through the circulation of the networks of virtual America. A "single" subject can be represented and moved through a number of different presents—presents made up of simulated versions of the past, or possibilities of the future—and in this way the notion of a fixed subject position is undone, cut loose. Authorings of Marilyn claim to reveal the "true" subject, yet each new book or image will be followed by even more "final" rememberings. We stand in the 1990s surrounded by images of Marilyn from the 1940s, 50s, and 60s. These images are not frozen in the past, but rather are often reconstructed in relationship to contemporary products, events, and icons. The fragmented subject allows for a dislocation and relocation of the present through the circulation of an image that collapses notions of subjects frozen in linear time. Now a history, an identity, a moment is reproduced through the person of the icon, radiating out from her body and image.

In the body of her political cultural reproduction, Marilyn is broken into competing "whole, real, true" rememberings, each of which claims to tell the true story, to approach the real woman, to present a final solution to the Marilyn problem. A haunting form of democracy emerges in the land of phantoms where Marilyn is remembered again and again one last time: every truth seems possible, every body is a site where Marilyn may appear to live. Yes, even the great can be rubber-stamped on the back of a letter, or emblazoned on the front of a coffee mug. Ladies and gentlemen, the late Marilyn Monroe.[7] Looking today at the

7. Marilyn was often introduced, "Ladies and Gentlemen, the late Marilyn Monroe," because she was notoriously late for all of her engagements. She appeared at Madison Square Garden while she was shooting *Something's Got to Give,* missing time on the film for Kennedy's gala birthday event, a fact partially responsible for her later dismissal from the film.

grainy, black-and-white footage of Marilyn swaying on the stage at Madison Square Garden, singing "Thanks for the Memories" in her signature breathy voice to John Fitzgerald Kennedy on his birthday, it appears that her translucent body was already becoming the body of film itself, film's body, as she warbles a tribute to her alleged lover in the last summer of her life.[8] In the footage she seems already disappearing, gone the way of the vampire, dead yet immortal, a memento mori of herself. Years later we continue to sing these songs, thanks for the memories, thank you so much. And so an immortal Marilyn remains *in medias res*, figuring a political culture that appears to long for the full presence of a unitary identity, and yet reproduces the same identity as a series of competing subjects and objects.

Each remembering of Marilyn has added to her cultural corpus, fleshing out an icon who often stands in for America herself. She is at once the poor little orphan girl—America's lost daughter—and the great success story, the American dream made flesh. Marilyn died an untimely death, a death that, rather than lock her in the past, breathes life into her in the present, adding to her status as remembered subject. The death sheds light on the life. The life illuminates the death. Again and again we go over her words, her clothing, her remains. We reassemble her, recollect her, resurrect her. We recognize her in other people, who quote her: When asked if she had anything on during the nude photo shoot in which the famous calendar pose was taken, she replied, "Only the radio." These memento mori, these one-liners (Monroeisms) that click out like so many wire-service epitaphs, help us to remember Marilyn now and even unto the end of the century. Hers is not a unique phenomenon in the United States: our nation is an imaginary landscape dotted with the monuments, documents, and detritus of the dead and the living, marking our ongoing struggle with identity. Our multiple identities do not resolve into a single self, so who better than Marilyn to represent our identity problem?

8. I am sampling the term *film's body* from the work of Vivian Sobchack. For a definition of this term, see Sobchack, *The Address of the Eye: A Phenomenology of Film Experience* (Princeton: Princeton University Press, 1992).

The history of the United States is marked by an abundance of cultural identities that remain in tension with one another and within
themselves, and that do not resolve into a final national "whole."
Nevertheless, it is possible to approach specific cultural subjects as
they have been and continue to be made, and in so doing to approach
the narrations of nation, the rememberings of political culture, as
companion pieces to articulations of single and collective selves. The
sites for the narration of nation and self are many, and the common
grounds of constructed identities form the landscapes of the historical.
These narrations range from literary texts to artistic works, from con-
tests over racial and gendered identities to contracts interweaving the
social and legal fabric of our material world. In this book I map the
contours of Marilyn's constructed identity as a way of approaching an
historical landscape. Rememberings of Marilyn are not, of course, the
only texts that graph the American landscape, but they are particularly
expressive of the mass-mediated common ground of our time. Woven
as the material of fiction and politics, epic history and everyday life,
and fitted like clothing to the body of a dead woman whose stories are
repeatedly forgotten, retold, and challenged, these rememberings trace
the character of memory in our time. Ours is a nation narrated in
spaces hovering between dream landscapes and common-sense logic.
The sensibility that pioneers a life, land, and identity out of continen-
tal vastness is the same that gravitates toward the field of dreams and
meanings that is Marilyn. We cannot mine this field of dreams for the
one true body politic beneath the phantom images: we must remain *in
medias res* if we are to encounter the political cultural condition she is
made to remember.

Cultural remembering *in medias res* often combines figures from
different times, spheres, and places in mass-circulated images and narratives. So it is that a popular postcard of the 1980s and 90s features a 1954
photograph of Marilyn Monroe and Ronald Reagan engaged in what
appears to be a lighthearted conversation. This photograph could be
found on postcards in gift shops across the nation during Reagan's presidency. With the passage of time, the postcard had accumulated new
meanings and resonances: here they were smiling, young, as yet un-

touched by the changes to which the 1980s viewer was privy. The pairing of these cultural icons proffers a bounty of possible meanings. Those who ascribe to the theories of Marilyn's death by association with the Kennedys might read this as a reminder of the dangers of political liaisons, even as a condemnation of the Democratic party. The image might also be taken as a trivialization of Reagan, a reminder of his roots in "the movies," and a tacit challenge of his ability as a leader. Regardless of its meaning to specific viewers, this image is an example of cultural remembering *in medias res* whose importance lies in its confusion of time and historical content. Both icons are made to inhabit the common ground *in medias res*, together standing in for the country with which they are associated. The postcard is an iconic remembering of American identity manifest in a highly technologized society. Historical actors and actresses, the representative characters of the past and present, appear together in narratives that combine discrete time periods, social spheres, and expected roles, and are remembered into the common ground *in medias res*. Indeed, they appear together *as* images.

Such rememberings comprise the postmodern nation, a landscape that is both material and metaphorical, containing a host of sites ranging from television programs to social programs, from state-of-the-union addresses to residential addresses. The channels of mass-mediated representation generate this landscape—our political cultural common ground is that of the media itself. As citizens monitor the content and form of mass-mediated stories, or rememberings, they are themselves remembered into the simulated spaces of the postmodern nation.

Mass-mediated rememberings exist in dynamic relation to the postmodern body politic. From the use of television talk shows as debate forums in the 1992 presidential campaign to filmic recreations of the Vietnam war, mass-mediated rememberings envision the possibilities and limitations of political cultural representation in contemporary America.[9] As Guy DeBord writes in his *Society of the Spectacle,* "The

---

9. I use the term *mediation* to describe the processes by which figures, characters, and narratives circulate among citizens and through the mechanisms of the mass media in a highly technologized society. I mean to stress the dynamic

spectacle is not a collection of images, but a social relation among people, mediated by images."[10]

Mass-mediated rememberings, like DeBord's spectacles, express and mediate social relations among people. Through their circulation, they constitute cultural expressions of common relationships to knowledge, power, and identity. They do not capture a preexisting reality so much as they generate and express, through their construction of the world, the character of the real at a given moment. The social relations mediated by images operate in the space *in medias res* that circulates through a virtual American community.

The normalization of a virtual American community through the mass media has set the scene for representative characters such as Marilyn Monroe to enter *in medias res*. In mass-mediated political culture, a space of memory opens up that offers the possibility of democratic recognition and public presence, if only for a brief moment. For instance, rememberings such as *People* magazine and national and local newscasts feature figures from all walks of life, allowing us to see and hear the stories of the "little people" on a grand scale. These representations are not necessarily associated with the weight of monumentalized history, nor with the pleasures of popular memory: they configure some blend of the two, or introduce a new category altogether.[11] When we view stories of women soldiers stationed in the Persian Gulf on ABC's

---

character of this circulation by using this word. I use the term *mediator* to define the person reading the text, viewing the program, etc. I have intentionally chosen *mediator* over terms such as *consumer* and *participant/viewer* because I want to stress the phenomenological give and take between the mediator and a given production. I further want to stress perception and translation as fundamental processes of political cultural being transacted between persons and texts.

10. Guy DeBord, *The Society of the Spectacle* (Detroit: Black and Red Press, 1970), 4.
11. My deWnition of "popular culture" is roughly analogous to that developed by John Fiske in Understanding Popular Culture (Boston: Unwin Hyman, 1989). See my discussion of Fiske in the Introduction and Chapter 2. I particularly

Good Morning America, or read a *USA Today* account of a young woman who has been exposed to the AIDS virus at her dentist's office, we encounter a sort of "grand historical narrative" by virtue of the authority granted to these stories through the sheer volume of their exposure.[12] At the same time, we are remembering, via the mechanisms of an epic historical consciousness, those who might otherwise be excluded from history as "extras." Of course, these extras tend to disappear quickly from the virtual American community, as each is replaced by a steady stream of new representative types made to convey values, relay disasters, illustrate lessons, and humanize issues. Representative characters such as Marilyn Monroe allow for some familiarity in the virtual American community.

By virtue of her familiarity, Marilyn serves as a sort of cultural currency—the coin of the real. Her name may be invoked by guests on talk shows, newspaper reporters, political commentators, and other actors as an instantly recognizable expression of a mood, an era, a sexuality; in short, she allows an audience to draw from a common ground of mem-

---

emphasize his initial discussion of popular culture on pp. 23–26 of his text, in which he argues that popular culture is evidenced and produced in contemporary society through allegiances, transformations, and identifcations made by consumers with mass-produced commodities. As noted in the Introduction, however, Fiske discounts the possibility of mass culture as "a contradiction in terms."

It is at this point that I depart from Fiske, though not from his outline of cultural productions or his assertion that "people do not behave as a mass," but by making a distinction between the form of popular (political) cultural literacy and production marked through identification and allegiance and the form of the characters, meanings, and networks generated through mass-mediated channels. While these mass-mediated rememberings may reflect and interact with popular cultural productions, they nevertheless encompass and exceed "the popular" in more extensive and diverse forms.

12. "Everywhere socialization is measured according to exposure through media messages. Those who are under-exposed to the media are virtually asocial or desocialized." Jean Baudrillard, "Implosion of Meaning in the Media," in *In the Shadow of the Silent Majorities,* trans. Paul Foss, John Johnston, and Paul Patton (New York: Semiotext(e) Foreign Agents Series, 1983), 96.

ory in understanding the subject at hand. When Spalding Gray ends his film *Swimming to Cambodia* with the words, "Now I understand why Marilyn Monroe killed herself," the audience is thrown back to its shared knowledge of Marilyn's story. This is not simply a reference to the tragic death of a Hollywood actress: as a representative character, Marilyn evokes a mood and an era; she is "shorthand" for the confusion, mourning, nostalgia, and loss that Gray's film identifies as the marks of a common contemporary condition. Not all invocations of Marilyn are as elaborate: we may compare a woman's figure with hers, or we may mention her as the epitome of sex symbols, blondes, Hollywood, or fame. What matters is that Marilyn has currency, and so can be exchanged in these cultural transactions as a means of illustrating or negotiating a subject. She allows for the building of discourse in virtual America.

The ways we remember in the realm of mass-mediated political culture mark some of the possibilities and limitations involved in constructing our political present. I employ the term "remembering" in order to engage in a discussion that is not limited by genre boundaries. The language of memory is able to transgress the divisions that situate "histories" in one arena and "theories" or "ideologies" in another. This language goes further in dismantling disciplinary structures by allowing the simultaneous examination of both fictional works and "factual" treatises, both cultural artifacts and practices. A language of memory, as opposed to a discussion of "history" (or the role of the historical), corresponds to a model of political culture. By employing a fluid construction such as remembering, I stress the degree to which the transactions of political culture occur between persons and products as a form of world-making circulated and manifested through mass-mediation. "Remembered subjects," then, construct and mediate cultural epistemologies and ontologies. A series of disparate rememberings may achieve, if not a sum-total effect, then a host of representational possibilities for political cultural meaning. A language of memory emphasizes the role of the subject—both the producer of the text and the mediator of same—in the constitution of a past and present "real" world. Studying mass-mediated rememberings requires a broad and dynamic understanding of the varied forms of storytelling and imaging at work and play in the ongoing production of a political cultural order.

In a society in which mass-mediated rememberings are commonplace, the media shift the site of "communities of memory" from lived historical experience to a virtual common ground. Mass-mediated modes of remembering express a number of possibilities of political cultural life in late-twentieth-century America. They convey definitions of action and heroism, models of history, and modes of writing; they relay terms of success and failure, roles of masculinity and femininity, networks of power and knowledge, and relationships to time and place. The ubiquity of mass-mediated rememberings signals the development of a field of political cultural memory in which community, relationships, bodies, and identities are translated through mass channels at an accelerated pace. The (s)pace of politics is reconstituted through these mass-mediated rememberings as a space of virtual performance. Representative characters help to make that space more navigable, to slow down the pace of a world so overwhelmingly populated with people and stories as to appear, at times, incomprehensible. In this way, representative characters allow for building and expressing forms of community.

Where does this community exist? Most Americans are members of this community: coming home from work or school, they hear, watch, and read the same stories comprising "the day's news"; in supermarket lines across the country, they peruse, however briefly, the same tabloid headlines and magazine covers. If they grow up in a home where there is a television, or attend schools with other children who regularly watch TV, they are familiar with the same virtual families, celebrities, cartoons, commercials, and so on. Of course, those who remain at home—by virtue of choice or lack thereof—are subject to the same stories. A realm of appearance is effected whereby hundreds of millions of people who have little physical contact with one another become members of the same community because they are literate in the network of stories, characters, and figures that populate the terrain of the mass-mediated common ground.

This realm of appearance is akin to the "community of memory" model developed by the authors of *Habits of the Heart*. They write:

> Communities, in the sense we are using the term, have a history—in an important sense they are constituted by their past—and for this reason we can speak of a real community as a "community of memory," one that does not forget its past. In order not to forget that past, a community is involved in retelling its story, its constitutive narrative, and in so doing, it offers examples of the men and women who have embodied and exemplified the meaning of the community. These stories of collective history and exemplary individuals are an important part of the tradition that is so central to a community of memory.[13]

The authors, Bellah et al., observe that "people growing up in communities of memory not only hear the stories that tell how the community came to be . . . they also participate in its practices." They term these "practices of commitment" because they "keep loyalty and patterns of obligation to the community alive." The authors cite ethnic and religious communities as examples of existing "communities of memory" that also require "practices of commitment." They add that "genuine communities of memory" relate not only stories that address the achievements of the community but also "painful stories of shared suffering and suffering inflicted."[14]

In mass-mediated political culture, communities of memory are formed in which large numbers of citizens have access to or knowledge of a common set of representations. These representations comprise the (virtual) common ground of contemporary America. Mass-mediated rememberings, however, do not necessarily require the practices of commitment that Bellah et al. associate with "genuine" communities of memory. Instead, they circulate representative characters as "examples of men and women who have embodied and exemplified the meaning

13. Robert Bellah, Richard Madsen, William M. Sullivan, Ann Swindler, and Steven M. Tipton, *Habits of the Heart: Individualism and Commitment in American Life* (New York: Harper and Row, 1985), 153.
14. Ibid., 153.

of the community." The community lives *in medias res,* linked across time and space through viewing, reading, and listening practices that substitute for what Bellah et al. term "practices of commitment."

Nor do these mass-mediated practices of commitment necessarily involve rituals that bond the community of mediators together.[15] The communities of memory formed through the mass mediation of figures and events obscure "original" location in time and space by installing the mediated simulations themselves as the common grounds of political cultural residence. Mass-mediated rememberings need not be concerned with distant or specific productions of the historical: much of what is remembered through mass-mediated channels is concerned only with the recent past or versions of the past filtered through recognizably contemporary lenses.[16]

Mass-mediated rememberings can thus conflate the local and national life of the citizen.[17] Citizens grow up interacting with the families of characters they come to know by watching situation comedies and soap operas, by seeing the stars of these shows interviewed on talk shows, and by reading about them in tabloid, magazine, and newspaper articles.[18]

---

15. One may argue that Elvis fans who regularly visit Graceland and attend Elvis conventions participate in practices of commitment that bind them to other "followers" of Elvis. But the "subculture" that forms around a cult figure has no specific geographical locus, nor is it necessarily related to the exigencies of daily life, nor does it require some of the conventional charges of community. For an ethnography and theory of microcommunities, see Richard Hebdige, *Subcultures: The Meaning of Style* (London: Routledge, 1982).

16. This eclipse of the historical is analyzed in Vivian Sobchack, "Surge and Splendor: a Phenomenology of the Hollywood Historical Epic," *Representations* 29 (Winter 1990), esp. 34–36.

17. This overlay is suggested by Benedict Anderson in *Imagined Communities: Reflections on the Origin and Spread of Nationalism* (London: Verso and New Left Books, 1983). Also relevant are essays in Homi K. Bhabha's anthology *Nation and Narration* (New York: Routledge, 1990), such as Rachel Bowby's "Breakfast in America—Uncle Tom's Cultural Histories," 197–213, and Doris Summer's "Irresistible Romance: the Foundational Fictions of Latin America," 71–99.

18. These categories of mass-mediated production and circulation are not always discrete. This fact was brought into high relief in the summer of 1994 when the

The representational community may bear little resemblance to the streets and life-styles of those who mediate its simulated pleasures; however, it is nonetheless navigable according to many of the conventional forms associated with residing in "real" communities. Citizens may talk about the events, persons, and subjects they've encountered in the representational community, using these subjects as representative characters through whom to negotiate values. The degree to which members of a virtual community can be drawn on as common figures through whom to discuss issues was evidenced in 1992 by Vice President Dan Quayle's criticism of television character Murphy Brown's decision to have a baby as an unmarried woman.[19] In making the character Murphy

---

O. J. Simpson hearings were the subject of a mass-mediated circus. Suddenly, a single iconic subject could be simultaneously broadcast on ESPN, CNN, ABC, CBS, NBC, and so on. Highbrow talk shows such as *Larry King Live* focused on the Simpson case even while *A Current Affair* aired reenactments of the crime. Tabloids such as *The Enquirer* and *The Star* ran article after article on "the Juice," claiming that he was being "squeezed" by an unnamed enemy, that his father was a drag queen who had died of AIDS, that his handwriting proved he was guilty, that he had a cocaine problem, etc. At the same time, the covers of *Time, Newsweek, Sports Illustrated,* and a number of other magazines featured images of the Juice in the courtroom. TNT sold highlights of the hearings complete with the Ford Bronco chase for $29.95, as reported in a July 14, 1994, *New York Times* article about what to do for "O. J. withdrawal" during the empty weeks between the hearing and the trial. Instantly, the Simpson murders were the subject of every mass-mediated category imaginable, including discussions of the media's role in the case. The defense argued that media saturation would make for an unfair trial; however, they argued this on TV. I am writing a longer piece analyzing the Simpson case. Suffice it here to say that it aptly illustrates the simulated fields of virtual America, even while it allows us to witness the reconfiguration of specific media categories, sites of interpretation and production, and so on. At the same time, it raises a series of disturbing issues in relation to race, class, and gender as they relate to and determine the content and form of media narration and iconic historical processes.

19. For media background on this incident, see Eleanor Clift, "The Murphy Brown Policy," *Newsweek,* June 1, 1992, or Lance Morrow, "But Seriously, Folks . . . Dan Quayle's wacky attack on TV's Murphy Brown character obscures a serious discussion about motherhood, morality, and government's responsibility," *Time,* June 1, 1992.

Brown responsible for the character and values of the American family, Quayle evinced the confusion of representation with "reality" endemic to the virtual community. Murphy Brown was "someone everyone knew" and thus she could be publicly shamed, like Hester Prynne, in an attempt to discipline a community sanctioning her illegitimate form of reproduction.[20] Narrations of the nation and contestations over its shape and future could be played out on the representative character of Murphy Brown through her discipline, punishment, and defense by other "community" members. (The same is true of Marilyn Monroe. In the next four chapters, I consider the ways in which rememberings of Marilyn seek to discipline, reconstruct, save, punish, and contain her.)

The constant and dynamic presence of the virtual community in daily life unites and defends "America" through a common ground of shared icons, plots, and figures. It is not just the representative character who is written into the body politic; the citizen, too, is written in. But whereas the representative character *becomes* the body politic through processes of cultural remembering, the citizen is written *against* the body politic through mediations of the representative character. Mass-mediated representative characters incorporate citizens into a representational nation, enabling them to interact with a virtual community. American people may relate histories, make sense of moral dilemmas, and negotiate their identities in relation to this virtual, mass-mediated community. This commonality allows the postmodern citizen the potential to make connections grounded in virtual spaces and figures with any other resident of "America." Rather than simply displacing the "literal" or physi-

20. Prior to mass-mediated narrations of the nation, literature provided the spaces in which contestations of the nation were written. For further discussions of *The Scarlet Letter* as a text about the American character and as the locus for political figurations of America, see Sacvan Berkovitch, "Hawthorne's A— Morality of Compromise," in Philip Fisher, ed., *The New American Studies: Essays from Representations* (Berkeley: University of California Press, 1991), 43–69, and Jonathan Arac, "The Politics of the Scarlet Letter," in Sacvan Berkovitch and Myra Jehlen, eds., *Ideology and American Literature* (London, New York: Cambridge University Press, 1986).

cal environment, mass-mediated common grounds collapse the literal into the representational. The mass media represent a body politic that corresponds to the narration of the nation: battles over the state of the real are waged on the common ground of the media. These mass-mediated battles range from the coverage—or lack thereof—of the Gulf War to controversies over the content and form of popular films.[21] In these debates, the site of the nation is itself contested: the narration of the common ground marks a battle over what makes up the common ground.

Mass-mediated rememberings signal the reconfiguration of the polis as the simulated "realm of appearance." It is in the polis that human beings appear before one another to constitute their world.[22] In a highly technologized society, people appear to one another not in assembly or at the courts but through mass-mediated networks—radios, newspapers, televisions, computers, telephones. If history is remembered in such a way as to bring the polis into being, then mass-mediated political culture coordinates an alternative organization of representation, the polis, and the political subject. Mass mediation dislocates the space of appearance into the space of simulation. Hence, a person is given a "real" life, real presence, when translated through videotape or celluloid. The narrative networks of tabloids and newscasts generate figures who appear as "the real thing" because they are known to the public. The media is the space where people appear to live, a virtual community

21. See James Der Derian, "The (S)pace of International Relations: Simulation, Surveillance, and Speed," *International Studies Quarterly* 34 (1990): 295–310, for more on representational wars and mass-mediated sites of contemporary political culture.

22. Hannah Arendt's definition of the polis is useful here. She defines the polis as the organization of the people as it arises out of acting and speaking together, and its true space lies between people living together for this purpose, no matter where they happen to be. "It is the space of appearance in the widest sense of the word, namely, the space where I appear to others as others appear to me, where men exist not merely like other living or inanimate things but make their appearance explicitly." Hannah Arendt, *The Human Condition* (Chicago: University of Chicago Press, 1958), 177.

where "men make their appearance explicitly," allowing individuals a common relationship to the body politic in our time.

As I stated at the outset of this chapter, some of the people "living" in the virtual realm of appearance are materially dead. The dead are some of the most powerful figures in the virtual realm, with Marilyn Monroe, Elvis Presley, JFK, Martin Luther King, Jr., and Malcolm X among their American ranks. They are members of a navigable community that contemporary Americans can refer to in conversation and writing as a way of discussing a range of cultural issues and meanings. These remembered figures mediate the character of the real in our time, as they allow for a hybridized realm of appearance in which the real is wrought in terms of simulation. The identities we understand, articulate, and perform in our daily lives are effected by the reproductions of "reality" disseminated through mass media. Mass-mediated rememberings transform the possibilities of public speech and action, enabling citizens to participate in a process of world-making in narrative form. Consequently, most Americans have what might be called "memories" of mass-mediated lives they have never "lived." They are familiar with the intimate details of a host of figures whom they will never approach in nonrepresentational forums. Mass mediations of political culture produce conditions under which a host of figures and stories once unknown to most Americans are now available to those same Americans as everyday "real" presences. The virtual common ground creates small, navigable communities of memory and meaning around mass-mediated representative characters, "neighborhoods" where citizens may live just as they do in their physical places of residence.

The president of the 1980s was himself a character representative of simulated rememberings, confusing memories of lives he'd lived in the "reel world" with the life he was living in the material world.[23] Not only

---

23. Michael Rogin, *Ronald Reagan The Movie: And Other Episodes in American Political Demonology* (Berkeley: University of California Press, 1987), esp. 7–8, where Rogin recalls that Reagan inadvertently called his dog "Lassie" in front of reporters and "told a mass-audience about the captain of a bomber who

did the body politic participate in the mass-mediated remembering of a simulated president, but the president himself recounted "personal" memories retrieved from film.[24] Michael Rogin interprets Reagan as a simulated representative character who is both situated in material events and is the material of a series of representations that feature his produced self. The simulated presidential character responds to and creates a political cultural condition in which the ground of the material is the stuff of simulation and representation. So it is that Rogin writes:

> The presidential character . . . was produced from the convergence of two substitutions that generated cold war countersubversion in the 1940s and underlie its 1980s revival—the political replacement of Nazism by Communism, from which the national-security state was born, and the psychological shift from an embodied self to its simulacrum on film. Reagan found out who he was by the roles he played on film. By responding to typecasting that either attracted or repelled him, by making active efforts to obtain certain roles and to escape others, Reagan merged his on- and offscreen identities. The confusion between life and film produced Ronald Reagan, the image that has fixed our gaze.[25]

In a political culture where mass-mediated rememberings have become the stuff of everyday life, the citizen's gaze is often fixed on figures who appear, like Ronald Reagan, *in media res.*

The appearance of figures *in medias res* does not place them beyond possibilities of interrogation and change. Indeed, the most powerful

---

chose to go down with his plane rather than abandon a wounded crew member—'Congressional medal of honor posthumous,' concluded Reagan with tears in his eyes—only to have it revealed by a sailor who had seen the film aboard a World War II aircraft carrier that the episode was taken from Dana Andrews's *A Wing and a Prayer.*"

24. The telling title of Reagan's first of several autobiographical rememberings, "*Where's the Rest of Me?*," was taken from his memorable line as the dismembered Drake McHugh in the 1942 film *King's Row.* For discussion, see ibid., 17–23.

25. Ibid., 3.

representative characters are made subject to constant reconstructions of their meaning, appearance, and place, reconstructions that reveal the nature of conversations about the present even as they draw on materials from the past. The constructions of the subject may take place as mass-mediated rememberings or as individual, daily practices of interpretation and identification. All of these rememberings index conversations about the state of the present political culture, pointing to inclusions and exclusions made in the greater construction of a national identity. This national identity—an American identity for the purposes of this work—is not resolvable into a final united state but rather comprises a series of contestations, disruptions, negotiations, and amendments. Reading the narration of America through constructions of Marilyn reveals the contested character of the nation itself: neither will resolve into a final, realized identity. Both Marilyn and America are imagined, made over, again and again *in medias res*.[26]

Battles over the content and form of the common ground of *in medias res* may be waged not only through the reconstruction of representative

26. The American project that aspires to make "of the many one" is predicated on forms of assimilation that often require a dismembering of past cultures and identities. In the postmodern nations of the West, collective terrain is negotiated through a host of political cultural institutions and productions that reflect the contested status of the singular nation. As the melting pot roils on, a series of resistances, antagonisms, and subversions points to the tensions inherent in any single national category. In *Nation and Narration,* Bhabha designates the narration of the nation as the site of cultural disruptions: "The ambivalent, antagonistic perspective of nation as narration will establish the cultural boundaries of nation so that they may be acknowledged as 'containing' thresholds of meaning that must be crossed, erased, and translated in the process of cultural production."

The "locality" of national culture is neither unified nor unitary in relation to itself, nor must it be seen simply as "other" in relation to what is outside or beyond it. The boundary is Janus-faced and the problem of outside/inside must always itself be a process of hybridity, incorporating new "people" in relation to the body politic, generating other sites of meaning and, inevitably, in the political process, producing unmanned sites of political antagonism and unpredictable forces of political representation (4).

characters but also through the use of a national symbol, or by challenging an institutional norm previously established as a "threshold of meaning" to keep someone or something out of the common ground.[27] As the nation is narrated on its simulated terrains, we must interrogate it about particular identities, events, groups, and so on.

The common ground of the simulated terrain of the media is beautifully illustrated in Borges's map of the empire, which Baudrillard takes as the finest allegory of simulation.[28] This map "is so detailed it ends up exactly covering the territory of the empire," and later fades, fragments, and becomes so confused with the original, or real, empire that the two are indistinguishable. Baudrillard takes this simulated terrain as the state fundamental to postmodern existence:

> Abstraction today is no longer that of the map, the double, the mirror, or the concept. Simulation is no longer that of a territory, a referential being or substance. It is the generation by models of a real without origin or reality: a hyperreal. The territory no longer precedes the map, nor survives it. Henceforth it is the map that precedes the territory—precession of simulacra—it is the map that engenders the territory, and if we were to revive the fable today, it would be the territory whose

27. Here, too, I am influenced by the thought of Bhabha, who in *Nation and Narration* writes about the role of narration in the evolution of the modern nation-state. He argues that nations emerge as a "powerful historical idea in the West," and that this idea's "cultural compulsion" lies in "the impossible unity of the nation as symbolic force." He continues that "the cultural temporality of the nation inscribes a (much more) transitional social reality," and that much of the ambivalence toward "the nation" is rooted in the discrepancies between the narration of "the nation" and the unrepresented lives, histories, and ethnicities of those comprising the nation. The creation of "the nation" through narration always entails the erasure or exclusion of some persons, histories, and cultures while privileging others. Bhabha sees the discursive site of nations as necessarily Janus-faced: "For the nation, as a form of cultural elaboration, is an agency of ambivalent narration that holds culture at its most productive position, as a force of subordination, fracturing, diffusing, reproducing, as much as producing, creating, forcing, guiding" (quotations from pp. 4–7).
28. Jean Baudrillard, "Simulacra and Simulations," in Mark Poster, ed., *Selected Writings* (Stanford, Calif.: Stanford University Press, 1988), 166–67.

shreds are slowly rotting on the map. It is the real, and not the map, whose vestiges subsist here and there, in the deserts which are no longer those of the Empire, but our own. The desert of the real itself.[29]

The desert of the real: a curious place to pitch one's tent, or to tell a story. Yet if we take the common ground of this desert to represent more than a metaphorical state and space, how do we then chart its political cultural terrain?

The consumption of phantom images is commonplace in the desert of the real, since the desert answers dehydration with the excess of mirage. Images alone, however, cannot sustain us: we must also attend to other needs that are as real to us as our thirst. Navigating the desert of the real, then, requires foraging for a language capable of integrating normative simulation with political cultural concerns—a language that both tracks the channels that mediate multiple hyper-present realities and is fluent in terms of authority, attachment, location, and human agency. Our thirst is for dialogue with the mass-mediated world dissolving around us. This is a world transformed by linguistic and theoretical interventions, a world where we can do more than re-view the same stories without reimagining their outcomes. So what can we do? Tell more stories, tell better stories, listen carefully to the stories that are being told. For this we need a theoretical scaffolding that allows us to map out all that is being said or justified at one moment. We need specific language. We need what the television screen needs if it is to make the world around us visible: sharper definition(s).

In the face of simulated political culture, a political theoretical discourse indifferent to attachment, location, and human obligation and relation soon becomes a dead language. Even as simulated discourses become normative, there remains the need for a civic speech that is capable of mediating between the citizens and issues of a community of memory, or of simply talking about the world in which it exists. In *The*

29. Ibid., 166.

Needs of Strangers, Michael Ignatieff speaks of the possibility of a civic discourse that attends to human needs in a postmodern society: "Our task is to find a language for our need for belonging which is not just a way of expressing nostalgia, fear, and estrangement from modernity. Our political images of civic belonging remain haunted by the classical *polis*, by Athens, Rome, and Florence. Is there a language of belonging adequate to Los Angeles?"[30]

As narrated and narrative space, Los Angeles is at once imaginary and immediate, and is thus representative of current mass-mediated America.[31] Though Ignatieff implores us to speak a language of belonging "adequate to Los Angeles," he is also suspicious of nostalgic and utopian constructions of civic selves and obligations. We are then confronted with the problem of creating a language of belonging that does not generalize from a single "nostalgic" and "utopian" remembering, yet somehow remains engaged.[32] The question is one of authority in and as language: where do we look for models of discursive engagement and participation in the expansive desert of the real? If the grand narratives

30. Michael Ignatieff, *The Needs of Strangers* (New York: Viking Penguin, Inc., 1984), 140.
31. For more on "Los Angeles" as city of simulation, see Mark Davis, *City of Quartz: Excavating the Future in Los Angeles* (New York: Vintage Press, 1990), chap. 1, and Sharon Zukin, *Landscapes of Power* (Berkeley: University of California Press, 1991), 217–24.
32. "Nostalgia" and "utopia" have recently taken on negative connotations, a fact that is itself an interesting American phenomenon. In Peter Euben, *The Tragedy of Political Theory: The Road Not Taken* (Princeton, N.J.: Princeton University Press, 1990), 13–14, American nostalgia, and Ignatieff's criticisms of nostalgia, are discussed in terms of the word's Greek etymological roots. Euben points out that "nostalgia" roughly means "the longing for home." He writes, "In these terms, nostalgia may be less an irrational refusal to adapt and adjust to a modernity in which we must give up all ideas of cooperative egalitarian self-governing communities, than a cry of pain, an instinct for cultural and personal identity and a refusal to accept euphemisms." Perhaps, then, a nostalgic or utopian language need not be dismissed as less worthy than a "realistic" language of belonging, if this longing is for a discursive home the same as that form of belonging imagined through "realistic" language.

that once "made sense of the world" are already coded as "interested po-sitions," then must we speak with a model that defines itself primarily in terms of positionality? Or is there some other way of speaking that al-lows for simultaneous distance and engagement—precisely the position of the person relating to mass-mediated culture. I believe that we have a model for discursive and theoretical engagement in the multifarious forms of the mass-mediated networks themselves. Virtual communities, virtual conversations, virtual landscapes all reimagine the possibilities of presence and absence, intervention and passivity in the contemporary world. A possible starting point, my starting point, is the maps them-selves: studying imprints of the virtual worlds left behind in the desert sand. Of course, this may mean that it is the world, and not the map, that we are reading.

These virtual communities may comprise a soap opera and its viewing audience, or a war fought with the help of CNN. They conscript mate-rial bodies, metabolizing them into themselves, and thus reassembling the body politic. They may begin with accusations of presidential infidelity appearing in tabloids and the *New York Times,* then move this conversation to a talk show. They ricochet from channel to channel, body to body, network to network. They are slippery, and so we citizens of virtual America must also be slippery. Not slippery in terms of escape, but slippery in terms of poetry. Push a world for all it's worth. Re-write it. Re-vision the image. Read and write in ways that extend the alpha-bet, that question what counts as the beginning of a sentence, that move around paragraphs, that see two words in one.[33] This kind of writing is becoming second nature in the age of the computer, at least for those privileged enough to have computers. Computers help to facilitate

---

33. The computer teaches us to think in moveable blocks, to scroll, to fly in mid-sentence, to put the end back at the beginning. At the computer, we see words as things that leap off of our fingers onto a screen curiously like a television screen, and we are both distanced and engaged. And the computer uses a shorthand of icons, which is something we are used to doing in mass-mediated culture.

Nietzsche's model of a gay science, a way of thinking poetically, linguistically, culturally, and personally while keeping simultaneously engaged and separate.

If a language of belonging is to make sense to members of a political culture, it must represent the plurality of practices and discourses of that same culture. Indeed, a single language of belonging could never adequately include all members in a given society at a given moment. To begin to forge languages of belonging adequate to Los Angeles, political theoretical discourse must look at those popular and mass-mediated articulations already extant as rememberings of our political cultural condition.[34]

Marilyn Monroe, the legend, is a wonderful starting point for such an expedition. She is particularly well situated in the space Ignatieff calls "Los Angeles": not only was she a native of Hollywood who resided there for most of her life, but as a cultural icon she continues to "live" in the virtual community of "Hollywood," or "Los Angeles," that is mass-mediated around the globe. But Marilyn's remembered form goes beyond a simple geographical location to the virtual locution of the real, which we experience *in media res*. As the dominant form of "public" discourse in America of the late twentieth century is circulated through the mass media, it becomes crucial to think about the ways in which these rememberings operate and the manners in which they circulate and pro-

34. Political cultural theory has forged "languages of belonging" for centuries, whether in the form of the utopian constructions/interrogations of Plato and More, the cynical sociocultural mirrors of Machiavelli and Montesquieu; or the social contracts and goods of Locke and Rousseau. A central task of these theories has been to speak languages that either resonate with or disrupt the practices of belonging in a given order. These theories and others borrow extensively from a host of written genres; they draw on historical figures and conceptual figurations; they craft our ways of speaking and thinking about political culture even while creating it. But they also change over time, even as they speak across it. As technologies change, so too do political cultural architectures: a theory that is to build addresses of belonging must philosophize with hammers capable of joining the residences of the real.

duce meaning. When we examine rememberings of the representative character Marilyn Monroe, we examine the discourses of belonging operating in our time.

These rememberings are not uniform, nor do they lead to a conclusive, unified subject. Indeed, were a "real" Marilyn realized in this process, she would lose her potency as a representative character. Much of Marilyn's power rests on her relation to construction: she is powerful, in part, because she can be made up again and again, in so many different ways. Her suicide is perhaps one of the strongest elements in the opening up of her possibilities as a representative character. Suicides reverse agency at the moment of death, giving the living subject a form of authority when there is usually no "choice" involved. Though subsequent rememberings of Marilyn have argued fervently that she was the victim of homicide, these rememberings have gained force through the initial naming of her death as suicide. This naming opened up Marilyn's death and, in so doing, opened up the possibilities—and impossibilities—of her life and meaning. It marks her as enduring cultural icon. And so let us read her being written, as we seek better resolution and sharper definition.

Marilyn doll and its maker,
Robert Seidenberg (1983).
Photo by UPI/Bettman.

One halcyon May day, long before smog, Vietnam, the Kennedy assassinations, women's lib, AIDS, and global warming, I briefly met Marilyn Monroe on the set of *There's No Business Like Show Business.* When she said good-bye to me that afternoon, she said she would see me in New York. But I knew I would probably never see her again.

Susan Strasberg, *Marilyn and Me*

She was goddess because of her force; she was the animated dynamo; she was reproduction—the greatest and most mysterious of all energies; all she needed was to be fecund. . . . An American Virgin would never dare command; an American Venus would never dare exist.

Henry Adams,
The Education of Henry Adams

Marilyn's human essence comes through in spite of the, at first, glaring colours, cold, synthetic, and unreal. A conflict thus takes place between one's reaction to the person underneath and the stenciled cut-out covering (metaphor). . . . Where does artifice end and the real begin? Is it the harsh contradiction of cold colours on warm skin? Is it that the accentuation of human characteristics is ugly, and in conjunction with a clown's exaggerated gestures, horrific? Apart from everything else, with her hair unnaturally fitted like a wig Marilyn looks like a transvestite.

Peter Gidal,
Andy Warhol: Films and Paintings

2   Ecce Signum

Marilyn Monroe, icon, is a sign of the times. The 1950s, 60s, 70s, 80s, and 90s are filtered through her form. Describing her first meeting with Marilyn, Susan Strasberg expresses a curious nostalgia for an earlier, simpler American era—a time before "smog, Vietnam," and so on— while simultaneously reminding the reader of the history that follows Marilyn's death. Marilyn is at once the seemingly innocent American 1950s—a decade that is already an iconic representation of itself, for its innocence repeatedly proves itself false—and the decadence that fol- lows. After all, what are the 1950s but one in a series of decade markers that communicate history in shorthand, media-style, for an audience who experiences the passage of time as representation? When Strasberg invokes the 1950s as an innocent time she invokes an iconic marker that mythologically empties history of its content. We now live in a world populated by images that live after history, bodies living and dead that serve as representatives of time.

Marilyn serves as both a reminder of the time in which she lived and an expression of the times that have followed. She is simultaneously the sunny, sexy, innocent cipher and the dark, dangerous, and disillusioned marker of an American legacy. In her various cultural incarnations, she assumes the traces of the decades in which she is reproduced, and her body is made over into a product of the times. As she is commodified and reconstituted in calendars, watches, posters, wine bottles, trading cards, and candles, she is reborn as the body of mass-mediated political culture. This body is so transparent as to be almost nothing at all, a flickering incandescence that sends the viewer into blank rapture. This body is ephemeral in and of itself, and so it must be crossbred if it is to live; it must be realized on the blank surfaces that litter postmodern culture. Every place is a place where an image might appear, where a cipher might be written. Everyday products are made to mean so much more as the image is poured into them, spilling over the edges of cultural production and filling in the hazy contours of a kitchen wall, a space over a desk, a television screen, a rectangular corkboard. The icon is loose, free of the very surfaces onto which while it is tacked, computer-screened, superimposed, photographed, filmed, and videoed. Suddenly, the world is a series of surfaces begging for the image. The image proffers presence, the suggestion of history, through its transparent body. The world is the crumbling church of this image, or rather, the disappearing and reappearing image has made of the world a mass-mediated church, flooded with the requiem of postmechanical reproduction. The image now and forever, even unto the end of the world: behold the sign, for unto you an image is born, and it shall appear as a body forever as a representation, a mediating body, a body of media, the mediatrix. In Roman Catholic literature, the Virgin Mary is occasionally referred to as a mediatrix, interceding between humanity and God. I understand Marilyn to be a mediatrix whose symbolic force is derived from the mass media itself. It is in the mass media that she makes her divine appearances and intercessions. As mediatrix, she mediates between the media and the people, while representing a brand of immortality which can only be generated by mass-mediated simulation. In late twentieth-century America, the space transmitted *in media res* operates as a sort of matrix. The Latin *matrix* refers to the womb, and its general usage in English has been to designate "a place of origin and growth."[1] As life and presence are granted by virtue of appearance in mass-mediated channels, so a public figure comes to life through the mass communications matrix. "Life" is transformed in the spaces of the matrix into forms of representation. A new hybrid body is born through the mass-communications matrix, and this body can live forever as an image unto itself. This is the body of the icon. Now Marilyn the icon lives forever as a represented character, embodying the possibilities for representation through the mass-communications matrix. She is a sign of power, conveying mass culture in a woman's body while appearing as a mechanically reproduced version of herself.[2]

Iconographic remembering is fundamental to mass-mediated circulation. Icons are culturally resonant units that convey a familiar set of "original" meanings and images. Because they represent content as form—Marilyn's image contains and conveys her "story"—they also provide a surface on which struggles over meanings can be waged.[3]

---

1. *Oxford English Dictionary,* s.v. "matrix."
2. For a discussion of "mass culture" as woman, see Andreas Huyssen, "Mass Culture as Woman: Modernism's Other," in Tania Modleski, ed., *Studies in Entertainment: Critical Approaches to Mass Culture* (Bloomington: Indiana University Press, 1986). Modleski also discusses the feminization of the mass media in "Femininity as Mas(s)querade," in her *Feminism Without Women: Culture and Criticism in a "Postfeminist" Age* (New York: Routledge, 1991).
3. The initial iconic representation of a subject suggests a "natural" form of denotation. The icon bears a resemblance to the object it is representing, and thereby appears to stand in for the referent—to operate as a version of the referent itself. Thus, the statue of the icon stands in for the subject of the statue: we may approach the being represented through the icon by approaching the statue. This does not mean that an icon has a static meaning; indeed, we know icons in part through their relationship to reconstruction and change. As an icon is remembered in a mass-mediated society, it is made to connote an increasingly

Icons constitute the real or the "natural" through their force as signs. At the same time, the changing characters and shapes of icons reflect the conversations and contestations of changing political cultural orders. An icon does not remain static; it appears in different forms at various moments. In the late twentieth century, mass-mediated iconic rememberings are often staged to facilitate the negotiation of the logic, content, and form of our representational orders.

Everything and everyone has the potential to be remembered iconically. For stories, figures, and identities to be transmissible as icons, they must first be compressed into units able to quickly circulate through the channels of mass mediation. I call these units *mediaphemes*. The mediapheme is the most common unit of communication in mass-mediated iconographic modes of remembering. I use this term to differentiate them from icons, which I define as circulated figures or characters that become the very surface on which other meanings are communicated. Mediaphemes are quick encapsulations; once a story, person, or event is translated into mediapheme form, it ricochets through the channels of mass mediation with ease. Mediaphemes may become icons, but they rarely do; they tend to last as long as a story, issue, or person is "hot." Icons, in contrast, outlast single, short-lived versions of an event, character, or history: they are the sites for repeated stagings of narratives, the sites on which the past, present, and future may be written. The mass-mediated mode of iconographic remembering relies on both icons and mediaphemes in the construction of the remembered world.[4]

---

large number of political cultural meanings. These additional meanings historicize the icon and reference the economy in which it is produced and circulated. Icons may be paired with any number of other places, persons, or ideologies to relay additional meanings and histories. For example, a photograph that features an Australian aboriginal holding a Coke is likely to connote Americanism gone wild, the expansion of the multinational, the growth of Westernization, and so on.

4. I use the term *iconography* to describe a process operant in daily life through the channels of mass-mediated political culture. I do not use this term in a formal sense to describe processes of classification. Erwin Panofsky draws the follow-

The icon, because it is easily reproduced, can be quickly remembered over and over again. The icon is a kind of stamp that can be imprinted anywhere, and when it is also a representative character, human form joins mass-mediated mode of expression, and hybrid bodies and identities are formed.[5] Put a Marilyn tattoo on an arm. Place a Marilyn bust on a bottle of wine. Name an album *Marilyn Mambo*. The iconic Marilyn is easily imaged, purchased, and moved; I can pick her up and take her wherever I go; I can buy her on the cheap, then exchange her for something newer, brighter, better. I can buy a new version of her when my Marilyn calendar's time runs out.[6]

---

ing distinction between iconology and iconography in *Meaning in the Visual Arts* (Chicago: University of Chicago Press, 1955): "Iconography is . . . a description and classification of images much as ethnography is a description and classification of human races: it is a limited, and as it were, ancillary study which informs us as to when and where specific themes were visualized by which specific motifs. Iconology is a method of interpretation which arises from synthesis rather than analysis. . . . So I conceive of iconology as an iconography turned interpretative and thus becoming an integral part of the study of art instead of being confined to the role of a preliminary statistical survey" (31–32). I understand *iconography* as a term for an operant mode of remembering culture under conditions of mass mediation. The iconographic process relies on a language that traverses writing and images, and that is able to circulate quickly through mass-mediated channels. As noted in the Introduction, my emphasis is on iconography's relation to other "graphic" modes of remembering. By studying iconographic modes of remembering in this critical context, one combines the "study of art" with the study of power, identity, authority, knowledge, technology, history, community, etc. The work I am doing here is more akin to that of an iconologist than an iconographer, to use Panofsky's distinction.

5. Not all icons refer to people, or representative characters. Indeed, we may encounter an iconic space/marker such as Hollywood; or an iconic event such as World War II. In this chapter I am focusing upon the iconic qualities of representative characters as demonstrated in mass-mediated modes of remembering.

6. Since I started writing *American Monroe,* I have received gift after gift version of the American Virgin. For years now I have been given Marilyn calendars for Christmas (I have three different ones for 1993), and so I have marked time, not with coffee spoons, but with black-and-white and colorized Marilyns—familiar Marilyns. She lines up the years for me, stands on top of my months, and

Mass-mediated iconographic rememberings are inscribed on a myriad of surfaces throughout contemporary political culture. They may be located on television screens or magazine covers, human bodies or plastic containers. Marilyn has been remembered on a host of cultural sites for some time. A 1992 *Entertainment Weekly* article reports on the commodification of Marilyn: "The huge machine spews out Marilyn T shirts, collector's plates, calendars, clocks, ashtrays, address books, shower curtains and hundreds of other items worth an estimated $20 million to $30 million in sales *every year*" (emphasis in original).[7] The authors of the *Entertainment Weekly* article note that Marilyn is worth much more dead than she ever was alive. The dead Marilyn is copiously remembered throughout the markets of contemporary culture, though the Monroe Estate occasionally spurns product deals such as Marilyn toilet paper and "Marilyn Monroe greeting cards showing the starlet snorting cocaine . . . declaring that 'crystals are a girl's best friend.' "[8]

We use many icons to mark the passage of time in contemporary culture. From their literal place on our calendars and watches, to their

---

peers back at me in my office and kitchen, the two places where I keep time. I was recently given a Marilyn checkbook cover, which I have been experimenting with using. Now as I total the costs of the month, the week, the day, I must first confront her and open her up. The circulation of Marilyn is not limited to time and money, as I am often reminded by my slew of gift Marilyn key chains, Marilyn is my entry pass to and from my work and my home. She marks my circulation through culture.

7. Benjamin Svetky and Ty Burr, "The Ghost and the Machine: Marilyn Monroe lives on in our souls—and in our T-shirts and wine," *Entertainment Weekly* 130 (August 7, 1992): 10.

8. See David Margolick, "A Courtroom Drama—Cashing in on Marilyn," *New York Times,* July 21, 1989. Margolick reports that Marilyn's heirs—now represented by the Anna Freud Center, the Roger Richman agency, and Paula Strasberg—are at odds over how best to sell Marilyn. Interestingly, the Roger Richman agency also represents the heirs of Sigmund Freud and Albert Einstein. With Marilyn Monroe added to these mass-mediated icons, a postmodern trinity emerges from the past as iconic commodity, as remembered representative character *par excellence.* The heirs make their living by trading in images of the dead.

figurative appearances in film, television, and print media, a host of icons forms a filter through which we mark location and place. This iconographic marking of time is demonstrated by a 1993 line of greeting cards, which begin with the year 1935 and continue to the present. Each year is denoted in bold, black letters on the top of its card; beneath it are featured a series of images marking important events. In 1955, for example, Marilyn holds the *Seven Year Itch* pose, with a caption proclaiming the film as "the smash of the year." Also featured are several images of James Dean: "[He] was the first teenager . . . too fast to live, too young to die. Dead at 24 and a legend already . . ." The inside of the card lists other 1955 events, including the death of Einstein and the redesigning of the Coke bottle.[9] The cards offer an iconic lesson in history. History is now the stuff of icons, to be sold as a surface of exchange and inscription for the cultural mediator to fill in and send off. The icon—in this case, Marilyn—is the term defining the exchange.

Our time is populated by iconic signs, many of them mythicized popular cultural figures. James Dean, Marilyn Monroe, Elvis Presley, Elizabeth Taylor, Michael Jackson, O. J. Simpson—each of these icons expresses a different meaning and mode of organizing culture, of remembering a time or place. They operate as shorthand for a series of meanings: early death, glamour, dissipation, isolation, triumph, youth, fame, domestic violence, racial identity, etc.[10] At the same time, they

9. Cards made by Blackwood Publishing, 22 Bridge Street, Walton-on-Thames, England.

10. My use of the term *icon* is related to, but not the equivalent of, Charles S. Peirce's designation of three signs: icons, indices, and symbols. For Peirce, "A sign may be iconic, that is, may represent its object mainly by its similarity, no matter what its mode of being." Charles S. Peirce, *The Philosophical Writings of Peirce*, ed. Justus Buchler (New York: Buchler, 1955), 104. For further discussion of Peirce's icon/index/symbol trichotomy, see Charles S. Peirce, "Logic as Semiotic: The Theory of Signs," in Robert E. Innis, ed., *Semiotics: An Introductory Anthology* (Bloomington: University of Indiana Press, 1985). See also D. Greenlee, *Peirce's Concept of Sign*, Approaches of Semiotics Series, ed. Thomas A. Sebeok (Hungary: Mouton and Co., 1973), esp. 70–84.

point back to a particular representative character—a discrete biography. I understand Marilyn Monroe to function as an iconic sign often reproduced as an image or name to resemble the referent Marilyn Monroe. Of course, this creates an endless looping effect, as the referent Marilyn Monroe is constructed to convey that which is already an iconic being—a movie star. So the icon as I am initially positing it here resembles the object it represents, but that object does not exist in some unconstructed, natural sense. Marilyn the iconic sign enacts the position of the simulacrum: the sign represents the copy with no original.[11] Nonetheless, despite her ethereality, the very ubiquity of the icon Marilyn delivers the force of her representation.

Marilyn's iconic force is bolstered up by reproduction. Her image has been traced, photographed, drawn, airbrushed, painted, and projected onto almost every surface imaginable. While standing in line at the supermarket, we may view a picture of Marilyn "as she would look today." We may wear a Marilyn T-shirt with a pair of Marilyn earrings. Marilyn is often literally affixed to products associated with daily living —clothing, key chains, etc.—yet she is also associated with special occasions, appearing on birthday cards, or turning an ordinary item into an extraordinary one (e.g., a T-shirt).

The relationship between Marilyn's everyday and legendary qualities is demonstrated in a 1993 Gap campaign for khakis. Khakis, the pants of the everyday, are featured in relationship to three legendary figures: Norma Jean, Ernest Hemingway, and Gene Kelly. (Interestingly, two out of three of these figures are suicides.) All three are pictured in black and white wearing khaki pants that predate the Gap product. The copy reads:

> LEGENDARY. Paris in the '20s. Hollywood in the '40s. Legendary writers, actors, adventurers with style. All in their cotton khakis. Casual. Elegant. Khakis just like those we make for you. Gap Khakis. Traditional, Plain-front, Classic-Fit, Easy Fit.[12]

---

11. Of course, this is true in the construction of statues of gods and goddesses, which also may be understood as icons, and so does not depart from previous forms of iconographic remembering.
12. Incidentally, only Norma Jean's name was trademarked in the campaign. Hemingway and Gene Kelly do not have trademarks attached to their names.

The Gap khakis are "classics" inscribed with "tradition" by the legendary figures who we see wearing them in everyday poses. (They look just like real people! Norma Jean climbing a rock. Hemingway holding a cat.) The ad seeks to make the Gap khakis into iconic representations of a lifestyle that moves between adventure, the stuff of legends, and the no-nonsense aspects of day-to-day existence. The khaki becomes the historic material of a legendary everyday life.

The Gap ads are not unique in the manner in which they affix the everyday to the icon as a means of creating legendary material. When Marilyn appears on the cover of a magazine, when Marilyn is invoked by means of comparison with another woman, when Marilyn is associated with a text such as the *20th Century Encyclopedia of Biography,* she grounds the everyday material in a repository of mass-mediated memory. Marilyn's iconic signature invests the cultural product bearing her name or image with value, presence, and historical force. By appearing as her legendary self on what are often otherwise unremarkable surfaces, Marilyn the icon secures the immortality promised and delivered by mass-mediated memory. The goddess now breathes life into the gift bag, the jewelry, the birthday card. This immortality does not, however, last forever: it is a simulation of immortality, the locus of which is the icon Marilyn. In the iconographic mode of remembering, Marilyn lives forever and yet is always already dead. Living forever in simulation, she invests the everyday objects on which she appears with an aura of mystery. She gestures always to her constructedness: she is a woman that is "made up."

A fantasy version of Marilyn's rebirth as simulation was envisioned in a 1991 film. A *Sight and Sound* article announced at the time that Marilyn would be "starring in a new film, courtesy of a computer."[13] The film "show[s] Bogart chatting up Monroe at a cocktail bar, coaxing her to transform from stone back into flesh." She returns to flesh to touch hands with a simulated Bogart. Imaging technologies are fasci-

---

13. Benjamin Wooley, "Resurrection," *Sight and Sound,* June 1991, 72. See also Bruce Weber, "High Tech Film Casting: Death Is No Drawback," *New York Times,* March 11, 1994, B16.

nated by the prospect of resurrecting Marilyn via the sites of computer and film reproduction. One site gives way to another as she moves from grave to terminal screen (a computer icon!) to movie screen—the place where she was made to live in the first place. She is resurrected as image: her icon body is born in the sites of mass-mediated projection.

A 1987 advertisement for Memorex audiocassettes invoked the mass-mediated preservation of Marilyn's legendary figure as a way of promoting their own technologies of reproduction. The ad featured a photograph of Marilyn's face with the caption "Maxell. The tapes that last as long as the legend."[14] Here the audiotape as a site of reproduction resonates with the iconographic legend of Marilyn Monroe. An equivalency interface is made. Marilyn's image represents the ways in which legends are made—those forms of immortality corresponding to technological reproduction and preservation. Marilyn and the Maxell tape will last as long as the technologies of mass mediation persevere, and so Marilyn is made to represent the tape's lasting presence even as it records her being. The icon Marilyn has been "saved" by the mnemonic tools of the mass media—preserved through the same technological apparatuses that initially "made" her. The body rebels but the image endures; Marilyn simultaneously marks the preservation of the flesh as eternal image, and the failure of the image to recuperate the flesh.[15]

14. The long version of the ad read as follows: "'Wow!' the world said, from the very first time she stepped onto the big screen. And through 29 films she remained the delicious dessert of movie goers everywhere, and the very best part of every man's fantasy. Today Maxell helps you preserve her films, with tapes that are manufactured up to 60% above industry standards. So even after 500 plays her sensual beauty will light up your consciousness, just as it did in the early fifties, when the world first discovered the magic of Marilyn Monroe."

15. The presence of Marilyn's absence via her suicide/problematic death particularly evokes the failure of the image to recuperate the flesh (i.e., "being"). Though Marilyn appears intact and ever young, she also suggests her early death and the ensuing controversies. I discuss this topic in greater detail in Chapters 4 and 5.

Marilyn's iconic form trades in on the cultural value of her image, as is illustrated by the *Norma Jean and Marilyn Collection, Inc.* and the Marilyn series of *Hollywood Legends* holographic collector's cards, "certified authentic" by the Harold Lloyd Trust. Trademark upon trademark, copyright upon copyright, the rights to the reproduction of her figure are tracked on the "card of authenticity" that accompanies the *Hollywood Legends* series. When I handle the holographic Marilyn cards I am startled by the silver aura of their transparent surface: one moment the cards are shiny blank screens, the next they are colored by the world around them. The holograms radiate Marilyn into the eye of the beholder—after all, someone must be present to activate Marilyn's trace, to "jiggle" the subject in such a way as to make her appear. Whoever holds the card may call forth her shimmery presence as goddess of this miniature silver screen. She is at once nothingness, a blank screen, and a cinematic version of herself, a series of poses from films in which she appeared. Her immortality as Hollywood legend is a surface of representation under she disappears. In 1993, another series of Marilyn Monroe trading cards was released as "an industry first," with each case containing "a hand-crafted card mounted with a certified diamond."[16] The cards were available through the "Sports Time Card Company," but were explicitly marked as "non-sports trading cards."[17] Once more the iconographic mode of remembering allowed for trading in on Marilyn's image cum body. The content and form of the cards resonate with mass-mediated remembering, encapsulating histories and subjects in portable images reminiscent of television screens. Like all other matter of mass-mediated culture, they have no particular order but are containers of themselves: Marilyn cards may be shuffled, stacked, tacked up on the wall, kept in a shoebox, or made part of a collection as they are perused by the cultural mediator. In these sites for recollecting Marilyn, the cultural mediator engages in a literal and figurative version of re-

16. Text from the trading card packet. Thanks to Mark Rigby for remembering me with several packs of cards.
17. Okay already.

collection: the cards serve as surfaces for quick memories of Marilyn even as they allow her to be made the stuff of a particular collection. Featuring photographs of Marilyn throughout her career, the texts offer iconic lessons in Marilyn's history, a history made to collide with American history. For example, the text of card 55 reads, "A very early Marilyn photo, most likely the work of David Conover, the Army photographer who discovered her. Did you know? Conover's Hollywood based Army outfit was led by actor-turned-serviceman Ronald Reagan." Each card features a gold imprint of Marilyn Monroe's signature at the bottom of the photo, thereby investing the card with a simulated trace of the real Marilyn. When we flip the card over, we see MONROE in block letters, while the fine print tells us that the design has been copywritten by the Estate of Marilyn Monroe, all rights being reserved by the same. Indeed, even Marilyn's signature is a trademark of the Roger Richman Agency—everything Marilyn is iconic.

Perhaps no one has so successfully capitalized on Marilyn's iconic character as Andy Warhol. His reproductions of Marilyn explored themes of iconic resurrection and simulation in art, media, and everyday life. Warhol sought not to separate the stuff of art, media, and everyday life into separate categories and ontological positions but to incorporate them into a single political cultural terrain. Warhol demonstrated this theme in his reproductions of Marilyn, the haunting, clown-like series in which we view an icon who is at once beautiful and grotesque. Warhol revealed the mechanical nature of the postmodern icon by reproducing Marilyn's image, blowing it up, coloring it in, and displaying it as one among a series of similar images.[18] In his 1962 *Marilyn Monroe*,

18. In Roger G. Taylor, *Marilyn in Art*, (Salem, N.H.: Salem House, 1984), Warhol reminisces on the birth of his "Marilyns": "With silk-screening, you pick up a photograph, blow it up, transfer it in glue onto silk, and then you roll ink across it so the ink goes through the silk but not through the glue. That way you get the same image, slightly different each time. It was all so simple—quick and chancy, I was thrilled by it. My first experiments with screens were heads of Troy Donahue and Warren Beatty, and then when Marilyn Monroe happened to die that month, I got the idea to make screens of her beautiful

Warhol produced a number of the same images of the icon's head, coloring each in slightly different ways. This series of "Marilyns" demonstrates the reproducibility of any body, image, or event as graphic commodity and the redundancy of mass-mediated iconographic processes. These processes desire a subject easily imaged and recognized. Once imaged, an icon can be reproduced; once reproduced, it can be placed on a variety of sites. The icon is divorced from its context; indeed, it becomes its own context.

The original, even the concept of the original, is destabilized by mechanisms of reproduction that make the same over and over again, *ad infinitum.* Mass reproduction of a subject images the specific while relaying it as expressive of "a type." Marilyn Monroe is a type, a reproduction; indeed, her type stands in *as* reproduction. Here she is an icon *because* she is the subject of this repeated reproduction; Warhol shows us a Marilyn who radiates the power of reproduction even though she is no longer living. "Warhol" made Marilyn again in 1968, at which time he said, "I tried doing them by hand, but I find it easier to use a screen. This way, I don't have to work on my objects at all. One of my assistants or anyone else, for that matter, can reproduce the design as well as I could."[19]

Warhol's reproductions of the icon Marilyn demonstrate and deconstruct the iconographic mode of remembering under mass-mediated culture. He shows us a subject who is reproduced so much as to be obliterated through processes of remembrance, processes that take "whole" subjects apart and feature them as fragments of themselves. In his 1962 *Marilyn Monroe's Lips,* Warhol reproduces the icon's lips eighty-four times in two panels.[20] Here the icon is both more and less than the sum-

---

face—the first Marilyns." Warhol also produced series featuring Elizabeth Taylor and Jackie Kennedy.

19. As quoted in *Andy Warhol,* edited by Andy Warhol, Kasper Konig, Pontus Hulten, and Olle Granath, and printed on the occasion of the Andy Warhol exhibition at Moderna Museet in Stockholm, February–March 1968.

20. *Marilyn Monroe's Lips,* 1962, acrylic and silkscreen enamel on canvas; Collection of Joseph H. Hirshhorn, New York.

total of her image: we recognize a Marilyn who we know as the parts of which she is made up, so that even her lips become expressive of the icon, stand in for the icon. The excessive commodification explored and exploded by Warhol confronts the viewer with a series of grinning, disembodied lips that can appear as either a smile or a grimace. This resurrection is fully contained in the realm of the image as commodity: reproduction occurs in such a manner as to kill or at least disembody its subject. The mute lips cannot address the viewer, yet in their silence they speak worlds about the force of iconographic reproduction. Copy upon copy, the lips mouth the possible horrors that attend the pleasures of iconographic reproduction. They allow the viewer to participate in the textures of mass production as an aesthetic experience even as they chide the viewer for partaking in that experience. As art is commodified, so, too, is culture commodified: there is no pure terrain of production and memory apart from the mass-produced images of mass-mediated political culture. Nevertheless, this culture becomes a thing curiously beautiful in its excessive production of people, products, and images. The excessive production becomes a sort of passion, a triumphant humor. From the many incarnations of the Campbell soup cans to the *Saturday Disasters* to the face(s) of Marilyn Monroe, Warhol injects an ironic edge into his reproductions of the daily as the stuff of late-twentieth-century iconic art.

   This art is perfectly suited to its subsequent reproduction as postcard; reproduction and copyright make up two sides of this coin of cultural circulation and exchange.[21] Now we may write a note on the back of Marilyn, via Warhol, and send it across time and space to convey its message. And the reproduction and circulation of this icon as artistic type

---

21. The postcards now read: "*Marilyn* 1967. Andy Warhol. Screenprint on paper. 36″ × 36″. From a portfolio of 10 prints. *Nouvelles Images S.A.* Éditeurs. 45700 Lombreuil, France. Offset printed in France. First Edition. © 1989 The Estate and Foundation of *Andy Warhol.* Used under license from Schlaifer Nance & Co., Inc., Atlanta, GA, USA, All Rights Reserved." Each of these "authentic" (i.e., Warhol) Marilyn postcards also bears a faint gray circular stamp on the writing side that reads "AUTHORIZED BY THE ANDY WARHOL FOUNDATION FOR THE VISUAL ARTS."

doesn't stop with Warhol. A 1988 piece by Paul Giovanopouls, *Norma Jean Baker—Sex Goddess,* now also available as postcard,[22] draws on Warhol's method in its reproduction of the iconic subject. In this piece, Marilyn is reproduced as twenty-five different figures portrayed using the formal techniques of pointillism, cubism, and realism. (The piece also features a Warhol-like reproduction of Marilyn, directly quoting Warhol.) Marilyn is shown to be not only a construction herself but also a constructed space demonstrative of iconic reproduction and its possibilities of construction. She allows us to envision forms of artistic reproduction under increasingly pervasive conditions of mass mediation.

The Warhol rememberings of Marilyn underline the degree to which the icon is made to represent a cultural type. This type may be reproduced, colored, and altered by other media and forms—even as other people. An August 1987 issue of *HOLLYWOOD: Then and Now* featured "The Ultimate Marilyn Tribute!" A special section headlined "Marilyn and the Hollywood Blondes" displayed photographs of "The Other Monroe Girls," copycat blondes like Jayne Mansfield, Diana Dors, and Mamie Van Doren, all of whom are portrayed as studio responses to "the Monroe type" during the star's lifetime. The magazine also included a list of "actresses who have played MM" after Marilyn's death. As Marilyn performed herself, others may now perform themselves as versions of the icon. From Hollywood actresses to female impersonators, those who partake in performances of Marilyn's iconic self/type replicate a theater of being already enacted by the subject in life. All of these types undo notions of an original self preceding the icon. Any body can be recreated as a type: the iconic character gives birth to the self as the product and producer of "types." There is no Marilyn apart from the "Marilyn-type," as the iconic character of her cultural being reveals identity as always reproducible, always a part of a "series." Now the copy performs as the original, even while undoing no-

22. Mixed media on canvas. From the collection of the Louis K. Meisel Gallery, New York. Information from a postcard I received in 1993, signed, "Lon Troyer." The penned text reads, "Greetings from Seattle. How else might I in-

tions of a fundamental split between copy and original. Reproductions of the icon stand in as the icon. The icon lives as copy.

Still, the icon has been resurrected as the "fleshy," the quintessential Marilyn Monroe impersonator, the Queen of Seeming-as-Being herself: Madonna brings Marilyn to life as and through her own body.[23] Madonna reproduces herself as Marilyn the icon in outfits, hairstyles, and mannerisms. With the name of the mother of God and the look of Marilyn Monroe, she ascended to the level of superstar during the late 1980s, forging her identity out of icons that preceded her. In several music videos she re-stages Marilyn's presence by replicating both her "look" and musical numbers from her films.[24] Madonna goes beyond a strictly visual identification with Marilyn to translating herself into versions of Marilyn's mass-mediated being. From "Like a Virgin" to "Like a Prayer" to, like, a blonde, Madonna has picked up the tropes of the

---

augurate my first vacation than by sending postcards to folks near and far? This postcard screamed you."

I would have liked to reproduce the postcard but it states that "Reproduction is prohibited." I wonder, then, how was the postcard made?

It is also worth noting that this postcard is not unique in its copying of Warhol's style. Among other postcard versions of the same, Marilyn Monroe is featured as a "type" who slowly turns into Sylvester Stallone.

23. For further discussion of Madonna's musical form and representation, see Susan McClary, "Living to Tell: Madonna's Resurrection of the Fleshy," in *Feminine Endings: Music, Gender, and Sexuality* (Minneapolis: University of Minnesota Press, 1991), esp. 155, 158, and 160.

24. She restaged Marilyn's "Diamonds are a Girl's Best Friend" as her "Material Girl" video, and she regularly poses as Marilyn in a slew of magazine articles. For discussions of Madonna that include remarks on her versions of Marilyn Monroe, see John Fiske, "Madonna," in *Reading the Popular* (Winchester, Mass.: Unwin Hyman, 1989). Fiske is optimistic in his reading of Madonna's popular cultural uses, seeing her as a site around which teenage girls and women may negotiate female agency and sexual identity. Also noteworthy is Lynn Hirschberg's interview, "The Misfit: Madonna," *Vanity Fair,* April 1991, 158–68, 196–202, for a photo layout in which she borrows heavily from Marilyn's repertoire of images. Madonna's recycling of Marilyn is evidenced in a host of other sites, such as her stage shows on the 1990 *Blonde Ambition* tour. For additional readings of Madonna as political cultural icon, see Cathy

three Marys, played with these Marian icons, and collapsed them. In one appearance she has the short blonde hair of Marilyn, in the next the long straight brown hair of the iconographic Virgin Mother. She swiftly manipulates layers of icons by alternately clasping a diamond bracelet and a rosary, or wearing one or the other around her neck. She is hybrid cum simulation, self-consciously reproducing as icon *in medias res.*

Madonna's intermediation of Mary, the Magdalene, and Marilyn is expressive of a political culture in which women are often marked as representatives of reproduction. Reproduction is figured by Marilyn and Madonna as simulation. Marilyn's simulated birth and rebirth as simulation make her into a contemporary cyborg/goddess, terms I have borrowed from theorist Donna Haraway. Haraway does not join cyborg and goddess as an expression of being under simulated conditions; indeed, she writes, "Though both are bound in the spiral dance, I would rather be a cyborg than a goddess."[25] I resist such a split in my understanding of Marilyn in her iconic incarnations as a version of the goddess/cyborg of mass-mediated life: I understand her as simultaneously marking the possibilities of simulation as a mode of reproduction—the

---

Schwitchtenberg, ed., *The Madonna Connection: Representational Politics, Subcultural Identities, and Cultural Theory* (Boulder, Colo.: Westview Press, 1992).

In "Like a Lady," *Esquire* (August 1994): 41–56, Norman Mailer writes of Madonna's relation to Marilyn:

Our love for Marilyn is not complex. She was our movie star of the Fifties, but Marilyn spoke of a simpler time, the Thirties. . . . Marilyn's horrors were kept within, and we mourn her because she gave it all to us and sacrificed herself until she was ridden with inner lividities and died. Madonna is not only a survivor, but has chosen, perhaps out of necessity, to survive, to take her kinks to the public. "You want to be with me, then come along for the fucking cure." She offers no balm to sweet, sore places; she is the stern instructor who shows us how difficult it all is, especially sex in its consummation. Yet she gives us something Marilyn never could, something less attractive but equally valuable; she dramatizes for us how dangerous is any human truth when we dare to explore it" (41–56).

25. I take this definition from Donna J. Haraway, "A Cyborg Manifesto: Science, Technology, and Socialist-Feminism in the Late Twentieth Century," in *Simians, Cyborgs, and Women: The Reinvention of Nature* (New York: Routledge, 1991), 150–51.

way of the cyborg—and standing in as the sign of force/reproduction cast in a woman's form. In describing the cyborg, Haraway writes: "By the late twentieth century, our time, a mythic time, we are all chimeras, theorized and fabricated hybrids of machines and organism; in short, we are cyborgs. The cyborg is our ontology; it gives us our politics. The cyborg is a condensed image of both imagination and material reality, the two joined centers structuring any possibilities of historical transformation. . . . The problem with cyborgs is that they are the illegitimate offspring of militarism and patriarchal capitalism. . . . But illegitimate offspring are often exceedingly unfaithful to their origins. Their fathers, after all, are inessential."[26] Marilyn is a cyborg reproduced through mechanical means and constituted by mass-mediated simulations. Her cyborg/icon body is often commodified, at times appearing as simulated projection as in the film described above. She is at the same time made to function as a goddess. She lives forever in death, and we appear to be unable to stop recalling her. She appears everywhere.[27] Objects and places associated with her, people who knew her, assume a mystical quality. We worship her in the way we have come to worship in late twentieth-century America: we reproduce her.

Haraway deems cyborg offspring "illegitimate," which, in the case of Marilyn, is quite literally true. She had no father, or no father who would acknowledge her. Her mother was mad. So in the end, Marilyn turned to the mass-mediated matrix and regenerated herself. She made herself up and we continue with the project. The cyborg/goddess is a powerful hybrid, the unfaithful yet faith-disseminating subject of postmodernism. Daughter of inessential fathers, she is simulated through a host of bodies, gesturing to the constraints of being under a mass-

26. Ibid., 181.
27. Anthony Summers introduces his *Goddess: The Secret Lives of Marilyn Monroe* (New York: Macmillan, 1985) with the following quote from Henry James's "The Wings of the Dove": "You're right about her not being easy to know. One *sees* her with intensity—sees her more than one sees almost anyone; but then one discovers that that isn't knowing her" (emphasis Summers's).

mediated economy while embodying and celebrating the democratic possibilities of the same.

The hybrid Mary/Marilyn as cyborg/goddess is one in a series of incarnations that destabilize traditional divisions between the human, the animal, the machine, the divine, and other formations and logics of discrete bodies and identities.[28] Marilyn the icon does not possess a human body in the traditional sense, nor does she correspond to a living referent. Do rememberings of this postmodern hybrid erase or participate in the mechanisms of power that accompany the creation and maintenance of unitary bodies and subjects? If the deconstruction of unitary bodies in the postmodern condition allows for hybrid forms capable of re-membering the languages of power that systematically exclude certain subjects while privileging others, then the destruction of such an "integrity" may be read as a politically transformative shift in the dominant representational order. But the question remains as to what sorts of transformations will be effected with hybridized figures.

Consider this case in point. In 1988, at the National Museum in Mexico City, the face of Marilyn was superimposed over that of the Virgin mother in a government-sponsored art exhibit. The substitution of faces met with angry response. Shouting "Mexico is Catholic," an estimated 100,000 protesters carried colorful images of the Virgin of

---

28. Haraway, "Cyborg Manifesto." In the section of the manifesto entitled "The Informatics of Domination," Haraway argues "for a politics rooted in claims about fundamental changes in the nature of class, race, and gender in an emerging system of world order analogous in its novelty and scope to that created by industrial capitalism; we are living through a movement from an organic, industrial society to a polymorphous, information system—from all work to all play, a deadly game." Haraway goes on to track this movement in the following "chart of transitions," which I have excerpted:

Representation	Simulation
Depth, integrity	Surface, boundary
Physiology	Communications engineering
Reproduction	Replication
Public / Private	Cyborg citizenship
Nature / Culture	Fields of difference

Guadalupe as a way of protesting the iconic de-facing that occurred in artist Rolando de la Rosa's work.[29] By putting these women together, de la Rosa was also taking them apart: his hybrid Virgin Mary featured an American simulation as the image of creation. Both Mary and Marilyn stood as symbols of reproductive force cast in the body of woman. Whereas the Virgin of Guadalupe represented a form of reproduction in which the divine body emerges from the physical body, the American goddess radiated the force of simulated regeneration over and against the representation of immaculate conception. Her immortal body emerged from the mass communications matrix. Yet de la Rosa's hybrid Marilyn was taken by the protesters not as redemptive but transgressive in a manner that merited direct action. If we allow for varied readings of the hybrid virgin created by de la Rosa, one reading must be that the hybrid imposes an icon celebratory of white, American multinationalism on an icon associated with regional, third-world resistance.

Margaret Miles's analysis in *Image as Insight: Visual Understanding in Western Christianity and Secular Culture* is useful here in describing the political cultural stakes of the iconographic process, particularly as set out in the tradition of mythoreligious representations of women. The struggle around de la Rosa's remembering of the virgin is one historical example of the transformation of an icon to produce a political message, a phenomenological condition, or an ontological statement. Miles understands many "symbols"—for which I would substitute "icons"—to perform this role in political cultural life:

> The first task of any culture is to formulate and make available to its members effective symbols, whether verbal, visual, or a combination of the two, for comprehending and taking an attitude toward bodily experience: birth, growth, maturation, kinship, sex, life cycle, pain, death.

29. The *San Francisco Examiner* of April 10, 1988, also reported that, "the exhibition by unknown artist Rolando de la Rosa, at Mexico City's Museum of Modern Art, has since closed down, and the museum director has been forced to resign." See also "Marilyn and the Virgin: Art or Sacrilege?" *New York Times*, April 2, 1988, A4.

Religion, as a prominent aspect of culture, must provide ideas and images that "keep body and soul together," that is, that enable individuals to manage—though not necessarily to articulate—a unified psychophysical process. The second task of culture is the articulation of the role and significance of particular individuals within the culture. Values relative to the interaction of people in work, commerce, families, and politics must be communicated in a way that attracts the support of a large part of the community.[30]

Miles designates two Marys—the Virgin and the Magdalene—in fourteenth-century Tuscan painting as expressive of political cultural relations in their time. She remarks on the degree to which the meanings of cultural symbols vary according to the perspective of the viewer because "a symbolic system will not necessarily function in the same way for all members of a community."[31] Miles contrasts the possible meanings of the two Marys for socially dominant men and for women, who drew their visions of biological life and spirituality from the same cultural symbols. She believes that the Marys mediate the transcendence of physical life through their renunciation of both bodily license and physicality itself, through their persistent representation of women as "image" and not as "person" or "body," and as symbols of freedom for women from biological necessity.[32]

Rememberings of the Virgin index the political cultural matrices in which they were generated: they illuminate imaginings of woman as the force of reproduction. The Virgin represents woman as both a material reproduction and symbol of a mystical force. She allows the mediator of political culture to return to the matrix of her regeneration. Miles is able to interpret rememberings of the Virgin as they articulate changing historical values and meanings precisely because representations of the

30. Margaret Miles, *Image as Insight: Visual Understanding in Western Christianity and Secular Culture* (Boston: Beacon Press, 1985), 82.

31. Ibid., 83.

32. Ibid., 82–93. Though I use the term *mediation* to describe her version of the Marys, Miles herself does not.

Virgin are subject to change. The iconic Virgin, however, always retains her charge as a sign of power—as the mystical embodiment of reproduction. Like the Virgin Mary, the iconic Marilyn functions as a mythical sign of reproduction; yet unlike the Virgin, Marilyn reproduces through the mass media. Though she gives way to mythic representations, these are mediated by her simulated regenerations.

Where the Virgin's transcendence of the body is rooted in the purity of immaculate conception, Marilyn's triumph over biological life is to flourish in an eternal youth of mechanical reproduction. Where the Magdalene achieves eternal life by rejecting bodily existence as license and sin, Marilyn receives immortality through the translation of embodiment into simulated presence. What was expressed in early modernity through two iconic Marys is reborn as a single potent body in postmodern America: Marilyn is both the virgin and the whore, the transcendent body and the seamy, sensual body. Reproduction for this Mary is grounded *in medias res*, in the simulation of the self as mass-mediated product. Marilyn gives birth, not to the son of God, but to herself as simulacrum. When we behold this sign of political cultural regeneration, it is Marilyn we find radiating both beneath and as the star.

But how do we address these signs of power? How do we approach so many Marys mediating eternal life and reproduction as they are themselves reconfigured, revered, and remembered? Mass-mediated rememberings of the icon Marilyn both deconstruct and reconstruct dominant frames of knowing and being in our time. They do not escape from the excessive commodification of the real in contemporary life, but neither do they simply reproduce forms of belonging for women that leave the dominant orders unchallenged. The iconographic reconstruction of Marilyn signals the ongoing struggle over women's place in contemporary culture, even while expressing the forms and possibilities of being under postmodernism. It is not surprising that these contestations should be so centrally concerned with issues of hybridization and simulation, for these are two overarching conditional frames shaping everyday life in our time. A "pure" subject or body, for which a single or original history can be traced, is a concept that makes less and less sense as we witness the forms of production endemic to mass-mediated culture.

(So, too, a pure gendered space for women, a nonperformative space, would not be fully adequate to the creation of an empowered women's place in contemporary culture.) At the same time, we must continue to interrogate the products of our daily life. We must interrogate mass-mediated icons if we are to read the possibilities of being, belonging, re-production, order, etc., that they outline. That a subject's identity is performative is not sufficient to a reconstitution of the dominant order in contemporary culture. A subject's forms of performance can also be problematic.

And so we must read the limits and possibilities of the roles our rep-resentative characters are made to perform. A potent icon such as Marilyn will perform many roles, bearing the traces of a number of au-thors, contexts, struggles, meanings. Her dominant attributes as an icon are expressed in the simultaneous presence of a multiplicity of selves. As these multiple selves, she both destabilizes and re-enacts fixed notions of gender. She is saved by technologies of simulation, even while con-stantly gesturing to her relation to simulation. She is remembered in ways that reproduce dominant orders and codes of political cultural power, even while some of these rememberings may be taken as index-ing ongoing struggles over political cultural power and place. She allows for rich possibilities of languages of belonging adequate to Los Angeles, while at the same time operating as an often mute sign: What can this dead icon tell us? She gives way to what is akin to a religious order through her mass-mediated rebirth, yet at the same time she expresses the failure of the media to fully recuperate her flesh.

We are a nation narrated by characters with double histories and hy-brid identities. What circulates on one face as sunny life, liberty, and the pursuit of happiness may flip to reveal a history of corruption, mishan-dling, theft, and loss. Marilyn is a bountiful icon because she expresses both sides of the American political cultural coin—the rich possibilities and the costs of dreaming an American life.[33] Marilyn's mass-mediated

33. Though there are countless other icons who also signify the lifestyles of the rich, powerful, and/or famous, I will note only one: the King himself, Elvis Presley. For a political cultural reading, see Greil Marcus, *Dead Elvis: Chroni-*

hyperpresence registers nostalgia for a "lost" time, vision, or country while stimulating possibilities for present and future versions of the same. In and as the past, she is the poster girl of the 50s: a fixed feminine identity in a legible representational order, a little girl/woman who promises, as Norman Mailer put it, to "make sex as sweet and simple as ice cream."[34] Marilyn is the womanly woman who represents, albeit playfully, a deliciously innocent American character. But in her death and resurrection into the present and future, she is the unsolved mystery of the early 60s: a suicide/homicide who lives forever as an iconic re-playing—a parody, even—of woman and mass media writ large in the American historical consciousness. She satisfies a certain nostalgia in both iconographic capacities, but a nostalgia that recalls the difficulties of the American project itself.

Consider the example of the hybrid Marilyn remembered as Madonna. John Fiske writes with optimism of Madonna fans: "Madonna offers her fans access to semiotic and social power; at the basic level this works through fantasy, which, in turn, may empower the fan's sense of self and thus affect her behavior in social situations. This sort of empowering fantasy is pleasurable to the extent that it reverses social norms, and, when the fantasy can be connected to the conditions of everyday life— when, that is, it is a relevant fantasy—it can make the ideal into the achievable."[35] Fiske's version of Madonna emphasizes her role as an

---

cle of a Cultural Obsession (New York: Doubleday, 1991). In his introduction, Marcus writes, "Elvis Presley's entry into public life came with such force his story was soon engraved into the cultural clichés that seemed to match it; the story became common coin because it already was. Birth in desperate rural poverty, a move to the city, first record on a local label, unprecedented na-tional and international fame, scandal, adulation; the transformation of a strange and threatening outsider into a respectable citizen . . . and then a slow seemingly irresistible decline: divorce, endless tours as lifeless as his old films . . . and finally early death."

34. Mailer, *Marilyn*, 15.
35. John Fiske, *Reading the Popular* (Winchester, Mass.: Unwin Hyman, 1989), 112–13. Fiske argues that only against the backdrop of "the functional common ground of mass culture" or hegemonic order is there a possibility for a subject

icon for empowerment in the eyes of her young female fans.[36] She defies normative codings of woman in simple dichotomies such as that of virgin and whore.[37] Simulation is employed in this fantasy as both playful and empowering for women. As women gain "semiotic power" by engaging in the tropes of Madonna's simulations, they may be straining the boundaries of gendered identity in daily life.

Conversely, the play of representation enacted via Madonna may be read as an expression and even a celebration of the sexually circumscribed position of women in the mass-mediated political cultural order. Rather than representing the parodic deconstruction of patriarchal structures, we might read the body manufactured by Madonna (et al.) as a familiar story of normalization and containment: she re-makes her-

---

definition that allows for the construction of positionalities (and personalities) capable of resisting or renegotiating mass discourses and codes. He writes:

> The necessity of negotiating the problems of everyday life within a complex, highly elaborated social structure has produced nomadic subjectivities who can move around this grid, realigning their social allegiances into different formations of the people according to the necessities of the moment. All of these reformulations are made within a structure of power relations, all social allegiances have not only a sense of with whom, but also of against whom: . . . it is shared antagonisms that produce the fluidity that is characteristic of the people in elaborated societies. . . .

> A text that is to be made into popular culture must, then, contain both the forces of domination and the opportunities to speak against them, the opportunities to oppose or evade them from subordinated, but not totally disempowered, positions.

In this formulation, the circulation of "the structure of power relations" through the mass media results neither in passivity nor radical reform, but rather a constant exchange of meanings that contains "both the forces of domination and the opportunities to speak against them."

36. Ibid. For a discussion of excess and its relationship to play, see 105–6; for his discussion of Madonna "wanna-bes," see 96–101.

37. For an extensive background on the politics of dichotomies/binarisms, see Eve Kosofsky Sedgwick, "Introduction: Axiomatic," in *Epistemology of the Closet* (Berkeley: University of California Press, 1990).

self into the "kind of body the current society needs."[38] Indeed, it is no accident that Madonna's iconic form operates as a mass-mediated tabula rasa, allowing her to stage performances of gender on a slender, white, blonde female body. Madonna's reconstructions of the self as simulation replicate a multitude of characterizations of woman that are "popular" in the political cultural economy precisely because they do not threaten the network of power structures that disciplines, displays, and contains the female bodies that do not conform to its normative orders.

When we think of Madonna's playful simulated forms, we must remember liposuction, skin-bleaching, dieting, "corrective" eye surgery, etc. Though race is introduced in Madonna's videos via persons of color, most of their racialized bodies are situated in visually and contextually liminal positions. By remaining the central figure, Madonna thus reasserts the American political tradition of demonizing and marginalizing the bodies of people of color, while affirming the figure of the glamorous Hollywood blonde as the central form in mass-mediated political cultural rememberings.[39] In the end, Madonna and her reproductions of Marilyn may be demonstrative of a flattening of bodies, identities, and histories into a shallow manipulation of mass-mediated being. Such blind ambition reinscribes cultural norms and orders even while appearing to feature marginalized bodies, persons, and powers.[40]

38. Michel Foucault, *Power/Knowledge: Selected Interviews and Other Writings 1972–1977*, ed. Colin Gordon (New York: Pantheon, 1980). Also see Susan Bordo, "Reading the Slender Body," in Mary Jacobus, Evelyn Fox Keller, Sally Shuttleworth, eds., *Body/Politics: Women and the Discourses of Science* (New York: Routledge, 1990), for an excellent discussion of disciplining female bodies into slender, contained unities. As Madonna has consistently reworked her body and appearance, she may be understood to operate in the grid of power relations that demand that a woman's body—and thereby her very being—conform to the contours deemed socioculturally desirable at a given moment.

39. For a discussion of political demonology and the representation and marginalization of racialized bodies, see Michael Rogin, *Ronald Reagan The Movie: And Other Episodes in Political Demonology* (Berkeley: University of California Press, 1987).

40. Some of these impressions emerged in response to a presentation given by Jennifer Wicke at Williams College, October 20, 1990. Wicke spoke eloquently of

Perhaps the countermemory of a simulated Marilyn might serve as a cautionary tale to the forms of mass-mediated regeneration associated with iconographic remembering. On June 12, 1989, Marilyn Monroe impersonator Kay Kent—a British model who had bleached her hair and "Marilynized" her figure using plastic surgery—committed a copycat suicide. A *San Jose Mercury News* "Parade" article detailed the dead Kent's transformation: "She did such a remarkable job of remaking herself into a carbon copy of Monroe that the Lookalikes agency in London . . . placed her under contract in 1982. Soon Kay, posing for TV commercials and magazine layouts and appearing at conventions, was the agency's busiest model, earning as much as $90,000 a year. . . . As her success burgeoned, so too did her obsession with Monroe. She studied Monroe's voice, her walk, her clothes, her smile. . . ."[41] This article also recounts, as did several others, that Kent had taken an overdose of sleeping pills with vodka, leaving her nude body to be found in her home. The role Kent had impersonated in life she eventually replayed in death—perfecting as simulation the end of her imitation of life. By disciplining her body and life to adhere to the contours of Marilyn's, Kent finally collapsed copy and original. She made herself a living body via a virtual figure; the flesh made media in a meticulously executed simulation.

Kay Kent killed herself by embracing the iconic self as her own. The role of impersonator reproduced for Kent an emptiness that coincided too closely with Marilyn's own—a role too shallow to be fulfilling. She chose to end her life rather than continue performing the icon's part; she took her life as the icon had. Even though Kay Kent was later resurrected as mediapheme in the mass-mediated remembering of Marilyn

---

Madonna's subversive character, particularly as expressed in the video for the song "Vogue." My colleague Stuart Clarke and I had an alternative reading of the representations of race in "Vogue." Rather than seeing the African American and Latin American gay dancers in the background as signs of transgression and political cultural empowerment, we read them as forms Madonna had marginalized in relation to her character and body in the video.

41. Lloyd Shearer, "Parade" Magazine, *San Jose Mercury News*, August 13, 1989.

the icon, she didn't last much longer than the cursory fifteen minutes of fame Andy Warhol assigned to anyone and everyone in the late twentieth century. Maybe fifteen minutes is what we can hope for in an iconographic democracy. Of course, when we consider the accelerated pace of memories and images in an mass-mediated political cultural economy, fifteen minutes seems rather generous—fifteen seconds would be more appropriate. It's a bitter pill to swallow.

In her own lifetime she created a myth
of what a poor girl from a deprived
background could attain. For the entire
world she became a symbol of the eternal
feminine.

**Lee Strasberg, quoted in
Roger G. Taylor, *Marilyn in Art***

In sum, the thing that was wrong with
Marilyn all along is simply that she was
not a man. She was too important not to
have been a man. Sure, she had male
virtues, her profession, her craft (and
something that is never admitted in these
accounts, but always implicit, possession
of sexuality), and these were what made
her great. But she was not a man.

**Dean Maccannell,
"Marilyn Monroe Was Not a Man"**

*Joe DiMaggio and Marilyn.
Photo by UPI/Bettman.*

3   Vita Feminae

Marilyn's life seems made for remembering. She leaves unsettled questions in her wake, a wake littered with photographs, anecdotes, "evidence," and impressions. Her life story is a play of representations staged by both herself and those who knew her, or who seek to know her. The writing of her life is informed by a number of questions, many involving her manner of death. Did she author the end of her story by taking her life? Was she killed by someone else? Who was she? Did "she" want to be "Marilyn Monroe?" Was there another identity apart from Marilyn that was somehow more authentic for this woman—that of Norma Jean, or some third subject position? Where was Marilyn's life lived?

I am interested in the life Marilyn has lived as a representative character. As such, she lives as she has been remembered. Marilyn the representative character is shaped by her authors. She is made to mediate specific values, meanings, morals, etc., through her life story and person. I am particularly interested in the gendered character of these rememberings: How do they imagine her life as a woman? How does this woman's life relate to the greater political cultural condition of which it is a part? What sort of an education is offered the reader of Marilyn's life?

From Plutarch's *Lives* to Emerson's *Representative Men*, biographers have aspired to write the life as a form of political and moral education.[1] In the chapter "Uses of Great Men," Emerson writes: "The world is upheld by the veracity of good men: they make the earth wholesome. . . . We call our children and land by their names. Their names are wrought into the verbs of language, their works and effigies are in our houses, and every circumstance of the day recalls an anecdote of them."[2] Emerson's representative men perform as role models for possible selves. As he reconstructs past lives, Emerson seeks to create the exemplary lives and citizens of the future. His task is to foster future human achievement by remembering monumental figures.

Yet *Representative Men* is not simply filled with human monuments: it is itself a monument not only of the possibilities for greatness but of a mid-nineteenth-century accounting of the great. Biographical rememberings index historical consciousness through the reconstruction of

1. Ralph Waldo Emerson, *Representative Men* (1850; reprint, Boston: Houghton Mifflin Co., 1988). This text illustrates the American project of writing the life as an education for the citizen and a model for making character the foundation of a great state. Emerson writes the lives of great men ranging from Plato to Napoleon, taking them to be representative of the possibilities of human achievement. Marilyn biographies might be understood as postmodern versions of Emerson's enterprise, but rather than being written by one great American such as Emerson, they have been produced by a range of authors. From icons Norman Mailer and Gloria Steinem to lesser-known figures such as biographer Fred Guiles and Marilyn's photographer/ex-lover Andre de Dienes, these biographers include both those who knew her and those who now reimagine her.

2. Ibid., 9.

representative subjects while also functioning as political cultural arti-facts expressive of the values, meanings, and languages of power deter-mining that which is deemed "representative." The reconstruction of the exemplary individual references the greater political cultural condi-tion and imagination that desired and designed such an historical and historicized figure. In Emerson's text, passages such as the following contrast the great individual with the masses: "The race goes with us on their credit. The knowledge that in the city is a man who invented the railroad, raises the credit of all the citizens. But enormous populations, if they be beggars, are disgusting, like moving cheese, like hills of ants or fleas,—the more, the worse."[3] Emerson's disgust regarding the "enor-mous populations" reveals the obverse of his representative men—the unrepresentative masses. While his project erects human monuments, it also casts the unexceptional, "massified" subject in the part of historical extra: one is either a rare individual or a flea.

Emerson's *Representative Men* illustrates an historical imagination that desires subjects who constitute the body politic through and as "themselves" or their productions—Napoleon, Plato, Goethe. Emerson demonstrates the greatness of his biographical subjects through the effects of their agency—they appear to re-form the body politic through their words and actions. Their lives are known and realized through what they produce, and especially what they make of themselves. They are marked by their achievements in the public realm; they are repre-sentative in terms of their "autonomy" or individual accomplishment. But what would happen if a woman were placed in the position of the exemplary subject—of the representative character? Emerson's model of the representative would have to be transformed, for the possibilities for making one's self as a woman do not usually correspond to traditional and strictly public models of achievement.

The representative woman's life is often articulated through its rela-tion to others. Marilyn Monroe's representative life has been narrated

3. Ibid., 10.

around and through her associations with "great men." She is portrayed as showing agency by manipulating men to get what she is so often represented as wanting: fame, power, an acting role, etc. Her sexuality, her sexual experiences both traumatic and otherwise, often take the center stage in these rememberings.[4] Her death complicates the articulation of her life in relation to powerful men. If she authored her own death, then she wrote the final chapter of her life, thus authoring not just her simulated self as icon but also the terms of her historical representation. She would then have exempted herself at the final moment from the relational equation. Yet even this assertion is complicated by later rememberings of her death as homicide, or by an understanding of her suicide as a relational action. Marilyn's death, it seems, does not resolve her life story; rather, it opens it up.

In *Marilyn,* Norman Mailer queries, "But why not assume Marilyn Monroe opens up the whole problem of biography?"[5] Why not indeed? What does it mean to try to write the biography of a woman whose name was not her own? Where should the author start—with "Norma Jean" or "Marilyn?" Is there a difference between the two? Do they even have a relationship to one another? Does the biography of the woman who became Marilyn illuminate the power of the simulated sign? Where does the real life end and the simulated life begin? Or does such a distinction no longer make sense given the (life) force of Marilyn's

4. This is particularly noticeable in biographies such as Hans J. Lembourn, *Diary of a Lover of Marilyn Monroe* (New York: Arbor House, 1977), in which the author discusses his sexual experiences with Marilyn in explicit detail. In other biographies, such as Anthony Summers, *Goddess: The Secret Lives of Marilyn Monroe* (New York: Macmillan, 1985), the star's sexual experiences and identity comprise a substantial amount of the overall narrative. I discuss this text in greater detail in Chapter 5.

5. Mailer expands: "The question is whether a person can be comprehended by the facts of the life, and that does not even begin to take into account the abominable magnetism of facts. They always attract polar facts." Mailer, *Marilyn* (New York: Grosset and Dunlap, 1973), 18. Mailer responds to "the abominable magnetism of facts" by creating "factoids" of his own. I discuss this in greater detail below.

iconographic rememberings? Which is the representative character—Marilyn, Norma Jean, or some hybrid of the two?

The young Norma Jean sits on the window sill of the Los Angeles orphanage in which she spends some of her childhood, staring at the RKO Tower, dreaming of becoming a star.[6] The anonymous child wants fame and a place in the dream city where she has no permanent residence, no stable family, no home. After her first marriage to the boy next door, she begins a career in modeling and the movies. She eventually rises to national and international fame, moving up from bit parts to starring roles. She is the blondest of blondes, the sexiest of sex symbols. She marries American baseball hero Joe DiMaggio and entertains the troops in Korea on their honeymoon. She later goes on to marry American intellectual/playwright Arthur Miller, to meet the Queen of England, and even to (allegedly) become involved with both the President of the United States and his brother.[7]

Norma Jean/Marilyn's story models an American dream in which the "American dream self" is the self-made woman. The humble origins of this archetypal self are reflected in her name, a name that bespeaks a rural American simplicity, that lacks a proper surname. Born in a suburb of the dream city, Norma Jean grew up fatherless, and eventually

6. For other versions of this story, see Fred Lawrence Guiles, *Norma Jean* (New York: McGraw-Hill, 1969), 3–45. See also Randall Riese and Neal Hitchens, *The Unabridged Marilyn: Her Life from A to Z* (New York: Congdon and Weed, 1987), 447. The authors provide the following Marilyn quote from a 1952 interview: "At nights when all the kids were asleep, I'd perch on the dormitory window sill and look across at the RKO water tank, with RKO in big letters, and light shining like a Hollywood premiere. 'My mother used to work there,' I'd whisper. 'Someday I'd like to be a star there.' "

7. This thumbnail sketch of Marilyn's life does not begin to serve as a full biography. Particularly strong for a conventional biographical narrative is Guiles, *Norma Jean;* for a large amount of data on Marilyn, see Riese and Hitchens, *Unabridged Marilyn;* and for a savvy take on Marilyn, see Mailer, *Marilyn.* Summers, *Goddess,* which I discuss in this chapter and the following two chapters, is particularly strong on the subject of Marilyn's marriages, as well as her alleged relations with the Kennedys and the mob.

motherless, quite literally a child of Los Angeles.[8] Here is the generation of what Mailer calls the "fatherless child"—the labor of a schizophrenic film-cutter giving way to an accident of grace and beauty: Marilyn Monroe.[9] From the back streets of Los Angeles to the courtyard of Grauman's Chinese Theater, Norma Jean made a mythical journey, imprinting her self in the end on the starry pavement outside of Hollywood's most fabled theater. The script, however, does not end there, for the failed marriages, the depression, the unhappy childhood relived, the early death—all of these elements combined with Marilyn's star status to grant the dead woman immortality.

Marilyn seems personally to have understood that her star identity was the product of invention, was in fact a dream self. For her, "Marilyn Monroe" was not a natural or "true" identity but a produced and constructed persona. In *Marilyn/Norma Jean,* Gloria Steinem recounts that when Marilyn worked she sometimes referred to herself in the third person. She reminded director George Cukor during the shooting of *Something's Got to Give:* "Remember, you've got Marilyn Monroe, you've got to use her." Before "changing herself into" Marilyn Monroe, she is reported to have asked her friend Susan Strasberg, on a walk down a crowded city street, "Do you want me to become her?"[10] The woman who became Marilyn Monroe appears to have understood the identity itself as a role to act—to have seen her life as Marilyn as a simulation of life.

Marilyn remarked on this double life in a *Life* interview shortly before her death: "People you run into feel that, well, who is she—who does

---

8. Guiles informs the reader of *Norma Jean* that the illegitimate Norma Jean was placed in foster care with the Bolender family by her mother Gladys, who worked as a film-cutter for RKO. Gladys could only visit her daughter on the weekends. Interestingly, the Bolender family lived in the suburb of Hawthorne. Perhaps it is in my character to see poetry everywhere, but I cannot help recalling another woman and her illegitimate daughter at this juncture. Yet while Hester remained with her Pearl on the geographical and figurative edge of the community, Gladys abandoned Norma Jean on the fringes of Los Angeles.

9. Mailer, *Marilyn,* n.p.

10. Gloria Steinem, *Marilyn/Norma Jean* (New York: Henry Holt and Co., 1986).

she think she is, Marilyn Monroe? They feel fame gives them some kind of privilege to walk up to you and say anything to you, you know, of any kind of nature—and it won't hurt your feelings—like it's happening to your clothing."[11] While Marilyn recalls the exclamation "Who does she think she is?" as a sign of indignation and dismissal, the question may also be read quite literally as asking whether there really were a Marilyn Monroe, or as casually assuming that "she" and "Marilyn Monroe" were two different women. This latter Marilyn Monroe was a cultural site where someone or something could make an appearance, but where no one could permanently live.[12]

It is curious that an insistence on and a search for the "real" Marilyn inform most of Marilyn's biographical rememberings. Gloria Steinem dedicates *Marilyn/Norma Jean* "To the real Marilyn and to the reality in us all." In a 1987 *Hollywood Studio* interview, Marilyn's stand-in Evelyn Moriarty insisted, "She was the *realest* person I ever met."[13] This insistence on the "real Marilyn" and her "authentic" representations aptly correspond to Jean Baudrillard's discussion of simulation and its strategic relationship to nostalgia:

11. "Marilyn Interview," *Life,* August 3, 1962, 32. Marilyn remarks in the same interview on page 33, "When I was older I used to go to Grauman's Chinese Theater and try to fit my foot in the prints in the cement there. And I'd say, 'Oh, oh, my foot's too big, I guess, that's out.' I did have a funny feeling later when I finally put my foot down into that wet cement: I sure knew what it really meant to me—anything's possible, almost."

12. Indeed, in the last line of the *Life* interview, Marilyn says, "Fame will go by, and, so long, I've had you, fame. If it goes by, I've always known it was fickle. So at least it's something I experienced, but that's not where I live." Where, then, did she live? Perhaps it is in an effort to answer that question that so many of Marilyn's textual incarnations have turned to her life story as a means of explaining or locating her true identity.

13. Michael Symanski, "Marilyn's Movie Stand-In Speaks," *Hollywood Studio,* August 1987 (special tribute to Marilyn), 14. Certainly we might take it as ironic that such an assertion was made by a woman who functioned as her filmic double.

> When the real is no longer what it used to be, nostalgia assumes its full meaning. There is a proliferation of myths of origin and signs of reality; of second-hand truth, objectivity and authenticity. There is an escalation of the true, of the lived experience; a resurrection of the figurative where the object and substance have disappeared. And above all there is a panic-stricken production of the real and the referential, above and parallel to the panic of material production: that is how simulation appears in the phase that concerns us—a strategy of the real, neo-real and hyper-real whose universal strategy is one of deterrence.[14]

The biographical search for the *real* Marilyn beneath the icon demonstrates the nostalgia that develops when the real is "no longer what it used to be." The real then becomes the product of invention. Myths proliferate, testimonies abound. Biographical rememberings function as authenticating "origin" stories, and "lived experience" becomes a means to locate, if not produce, a real referent. This "real" referent, however, cannot stave off the precession of simulacra identified by Baudrillard: the more the real Marilyn is recounted and represented, the more the shades of the neo-real and hyper-real encroach upon the real itself. The task for the political cultural theorist becomes one of identifying some of the stakes involved in these reproductions of the real, in the writing of these representative lives. What sorts of educations do they attempt to offer their readers?

For the remainder of this chapter I will consider two contrasting biographical rememberings of Marilyn: Norman Mailer's *Marilyn* and Gloria Steinem's *Marilyn/Norma Jean.*[15] Both biographers are icons in their own right, whose political cultural exchange value makes them singularly privileged reproducers of the Marilyn story. Norman Mailer serves, among other things, as the great American male, the icon of a brand of American consciousness conveyed from Hemingway to the "macho" writers of a new era. Gloria Steinem functions as the counterpart to Mailer's

---

14. Jean Baudrillard, *Simulations*, trans. Paul Foss, Paul Patton, and Philip Beitchman (New York: Semiotext(e), 1983), 12–13.

15. Mailer, *Marilyn;* Steinem, *Marilyn/Norma Jean.*

machismo; she is an icon of feminist popular journalism and a commonly recognized representative of the progressive or "new" woman. Each allows for an explicitly gendered reading of Marilyn's biographical rememberings that takes into account both subject and author. Both Steinem and Mailer have written life as a woman—as Marilyn/Norma Jean.

A Novel Biography

Norman Mailer wrote *Marilyn* after having been hired to do the preface for a photographic book of an art exhibit entitled "Marilyn Monroe: The Legend and the Truth."[16] His preface expanded from twenty-five thousand to ninety thousand words, developing into what Mailer calls "a species of novel, for a formal biography cannot be written in less than two years since it takes that long to collect the facts."[17] Indeed, *Marilyn* may be seen as the progeny of Fred Guiles's 1968 *Norma Jean:* Mailer states that it was on reading this book that he discovered he wanted to write not just a preface but a biography. Mailer based most of *Marilyn* on the accounts given by Guiles, and credited *Norma Jean* directly in both the acknowledgments and the main body of *Marilyn*.[18]

Mailer's biography never claims to be "authentic" in the word's traditional sense. He repeatedly stresses that he is not attempting to dig up the "real" Marilyn, for such an excavation, he says, would be limited and most likely false. His understanding of subjectivity resists unitary constructions of "self," as evidenced by his quotation from Virginia Woolf on biography: "A biography is considered complete if it merely accounts for six or seven selves, whereas a person may well have as many as one thousand."[19] It is these "one thousand" selves that Mailer set out to re-

16. Mailer, *Marilyn,* 257.
17. Ibid., 3.
18. Ibid., 257. Mailer makes no secret of the degree to which his biographical novel is derivative of other works, as well as based on his personal imaginings/rememberings of Marilyn.
19. Ibid., 18.

member in his novel biography. In the aftermath of the 60s and in the midst of Watergate, Mailer's *Marilyn* finds a simulated life to be a revelation of the real. The real is likewise not a fixed category in his biographical remembering. He writes Marilyn as a living fictional subject; she is a conglomerate of myth, simulation, and personal fantasy. Mailer also pens Marilyn into the incarnation of his desire, a "hollow into which he can lie down."[20] Even while he "deconstructs" an essentialized Marilyn, he erects her life as the sexualized monument on which he can mount his own subject position.

Contradiction lies at the core of Mailer's *Marilyn*. He even writes his subject as a series of oppositional forces:

> Since she was a movie star of the most stubborn secretiveness and flamboyant candor, most conflicting arrogance and on-rushing inferiority; great populist of philosophers—she loved the working man—and most tyrannical of mates, a queen of a castrator who was ready to weep for a dying minnow; a lover of books who did not read, and a proud, inviolate artist who could haunch over to publicity when the heat was upon her faster than a whore could lust over a hot buck; a female spurt of wit and sensitive energy who could hang like a sloth for days in a muddy-mooded coma; a child-girl, yet an actress to loose a riot by dropping her glove at a premiere; a fountain of charm and a dreary bore; an ambulating cyclone of beauty when dressed to show, a dank hunched-up drab at her worst—with a bad smell!—a giant and an emotional pygmy; a lover of life and a cowardly hyena of death who drenched herself in chemical stupors; a sexual oven whose fire may rarely have been lit—she would go to bed with her brassiere on—she was certainly more and less than the silver witch of us all.[21]

Mailer does not attempt to re-solve Marilyn by writing her as a single closed subject position; rather, he chooses to delve into the possibilities of Marilyn. His Marilyn allows for a multiplicity of identities, identifications, and historical narrations; she reflects the real with contradictions; she is written as a text that defies the split between history and fiction.

20. Ibid., 19.
21. Ibid., 16–17.

Mailer's remembering of Marilyn's life is founded on her sexual identity. He uses images of a "queen castrator," a lusting "whore," a "female spurt of wit," and a "sexual oven" to masculinize her sexuality while subjecting her to the power of his (naming) pen. Marilyn's sexuality is thus rendered in violent and often misogynist language. Her possibilities for sexual identity are primarily male-defined, as in "female spurt," or configured according to traditional views of women's sexuality and capital, as in "whore." Mailer's desire for Marilyn as woman writ large informs his desire for her as biographical subject. He achieves satisfaction by making *Marilyn* as both a woman and a text.

Immediately prior to *Marilyn,* Mailer had written *The Prisoner of Sex* out of a political cultural conversation with the likes of Kate Millet, Germaine Greer, and Jill Johnston.[22] In Peter Manso's interview-based biography *Mailer,* we are told that Mailer decided to write *The Prisoner of Sex* as a response to Millett's *Sexual Politics.* Other incidents involving Mailer in "dialogue" with the feminists of the early 70s are also recounted in Manso's book, including a 1971 "Theater of Ideas" event in which Mailer "took on" a number of feminists in a debate over whether "women should have their rights."[23] Heralded as both sensationalistic and the "death of the 60s," this debate stressed the tense political cultural divisions that were to become increasingly apparent as the 70s began—divisions caused and widened by "the woman question." It was directly after his participation in this discussion that Norman Mailer wrote *Marilyn.*

The photographic exhibit from which *Marilyn* developed was organized by Lawrence Schiller. Though Schiller and Mailer eventually col-

22. See Peter Manso, *Mailer* (New York: Penguin, 1985), 521. Manso's book is described as an "oral biography" based on interviews with a number of people who had contact or relationships with Mailer. His discussion of Mailer's debates with Millett et al. includes interviews with feminists such as Gloria Steinem. Manso reconstructs Mailer's life and his political cultural climate by talking to a number of the people who participated in events that included or were centered around Mailer.

23. Ibid., 524.

laborated on *The Executioner's Song*, there was a deep-seated rivalry between them over the production of *Marilyn*. Schiller recounts one of the most significant battles between himself and Mailer in the following manner:

> When I told him he was fucking up the book, Mailer said, "Don't tell me about book publishing. You've never published a book before." Then he said something like "Larry, you don't know a damn thing about laying out books." So I said, "Well, what do you know about Marilyn Monroe?" He said, "What the hell do you know?" And then I said, "At least I fucked her, and you didn't. . . ." We were standing about a foot apart, and while he didn't raise his fist, he was ready to take a swing at me, just barely controlling himself.[24]

It is difficult to imagine a situation in which the stakes of authoring Marilyn could be made more clear. Here we have an almost physical fight between rival authors, one a writer and another a photographer, in which the authority to "know" Marilyn flows quite literally from a biblical knowledge of the subject—he who truly knows her is he who "fucked her."

Such "knowledge" is strongly embedded in a phallocentric determination of subjectivity and objectivity. An "intimate" relationship with the biographical subject—or any truly known or knowable subject—is traditionally held to authorize the writing or making of that subject. Schiller and Mailer move from arguing about making *Marilyn* the text to "making" Marilyn the woman. Because Mailer never made Marilyn in life, he must now make her after death, going so far as to embody her in *Of Women and Their Elegance*, the text in which he writes as the "first-person" Marilyn.[25] Indeed, Mailer often explicitly identifies with

24. Ibid., 543.
25. Norman Mailer, *Of Women and Their Elegance* (New York: Simon and Schuster, 1980). This incantation is the next step in the development of the shaman's powers of incarnation: Mailer speaks as Marilyn, dreams up possibilities of a hidden Marilyn, and otherwise becomes his subject for the purposes of writing

his biographical subject: in *Marilyn*, he anagrammatically unravels and plays with his and Marilyn's names; visiting her cement imprints at Grauman's Chinese Theater, he finds that his hand fits perfectly into the she space left behind.[26]

While Mailer sometimes identifies with his subject, Marilyn also functions as a feminized Other for him, a version of the monstrous feminine—incidentally played out as a vision hostile to feminism and a hostile vision of feminism—which he must lay to rest if he is to remain fully himself.[27] Mailer relays a story from Zolotow's *Marilyn—An Untold Story* to demonstrate Marilyn's monstrous femininity. According to

---

a life. Mailer assumes Marilyn's form in his text. He speaks as if he is telling truths that he imagines Marilyn would have told had she spoken for herself. Whereas *Marilyn* is filled with photographs of the subject, *Of Women and Their Elegance* comprises a series of photos of women, few of which feature Marilyn. It is as if the iconographic/photographic remembering of Marilyn is no longer necessary because Mailer has assumed her figure: he has substituted his voice for her body, and he will move from a novelized biography to a biographical writing overtly named as speculative and fictionalized.

26. *Marilyn*, 20. Mailer writes: "For a man with a cabalistic turn of mind, it was fair and engraved coincidence that the letters in Marilyn Monroe (if the 'a' were used twice and the 'o' but once) would spell his own name leaving only the 'y' for excess, a trifling discrepancy, no more calculated to upset the heavens than the most minuscule diffraction of the red shift."

27. Mailer's obsession with the monstrous female, which is both Other and a taboo version of himself, merits further treatment. For an excellent discussion of woman as monstrous Other, see Barbara Creed, "Horror and the Monstrous-Feminine: An Imaginary Abjection," *Screen* 27 (January 1986): 44–70. For an analysis of the extent to which Western narratives are bent on a form of resolution that requires that the narrator lay to rest a female monstrous Other, see Teresa De Lauretis, "Desire and Narrative," in *Alice Doesn't: Feminism, Semiotics, Cinema* (Bloomington: Indiana University Press, 1984). If we take this Other to be for Mailer "the womanization of America," then his obsession and identification with Marilyn pose an interesting problem. She is both the body through which he authors himself—at times, even as a woman— and the counterpoint against which he defines himself. She is certainly a complex monster for Mailer, who suffers from a few complexes of his own. He is simultaneously drawn to denigrate and worship Marilyn as he fights to make her, all the while acknowledging that such resolution is impossible.

Zolotow, most of the cast from *Some Like It Hot* (excluding Marilyn) were watching the film's yacht sequence, in which a supposedly reluctant Tony Curtis is being kissed by Marilyn's character, Sugar Kane. In the darkness, someone asked Curtis how he liked kissing Marilyn Monroe, and he replied loudly, "It's like kissing Hitler." Mailer quotes the remainder of the Zolotow passage: "During much of the shooting, Monroe was reading Paine's *Rights of Man*. One day, the second assistant director Hal Polaire went to her dressing room. He knocked on the door. He called out, 'We're ready for you, Miss Monroe.' She replied with a simple obliterative. 'Go fuck yourself,' she said. Did she anticipate how a future generation of women would evaluate the rights of men?"[28]

Mailer's juxtaposition of Hitler as the foe of democracy with Paine as the champion of liberty sets the narrative stage for a battle between fascism and freedom. Mailer then takes Marilyn's exclamation—"Go fuck yourself"—and repositions it as a "feminist" interpretation of Paine's message, introducing yet a third representative of political systems and discourses into the equation. What sort of a progression is this, given the cast of the comment? Because Marilyn's "women's rights" are expressed simply as "Go fuck yourself," and this exclamation narratively follows her comparison to Hitler, we are led to perceive Marilyn as the dual symbol of democratic freedom/rebellion and fascist tyranny/dogma.[29] This hybridized body mirrors Mailer's fear of a hydra-like feminism. The ways of its reproduction confound Mailer.

Nevertheless, Mailer makes the woman who tells men to "go fuck themselves" into a version of Henry Adams's virgin Venus. According to Adams,

---

28. Ibid., 17.
29. A knowledge of Marilyn's filmography further compounds Mailer's textual irony. Just prior to making *Some Like It Hot,* Marilyn had finished *The Prince and the Showgirl,* a "British" film in which she had starred opposite Laurence Olivier as a commoner meeting royalty. During filming in England, the actress herself had been presented to Queen Elizabeth. As is so often the case in Marilyn's life, biography compounds biography as simulation compounds simulation.

In any previous age, sex was strength. Neither art nor beauty was needed. Everyone, even among the Puritans, knew that neither Diana of the Ephesians nor any of the Oriental goddesses was worshipped for her beauty. She was goddess because of her force; she was the animated dynamo; she was reproduction—the greatest and most mysterious of all energies; all she needed was to be fecund.[30]

Where Adams writes of the virgin goddess and her power, Mailer writes of Marilyn as *his* virgin goddess, his Venus in blue jeans:

> She was our angel, the sweet angel of sex, and the sugar of sex came up from her like a resonance of sound in the clearest grain of the violin. . . . "Marilyn Monroe's sex," said the smile of the young star, "will meet every human need."[31]
>
> Her stomach, untrammeled by girdles or sheaths, popped forward in a full woman's belly, inelegant as hell, an avowal of a womb fairly salivating in seed.[32]

Marilyn, like the Virgin, embodies the possibilities of reproduction. She floats as an angel or goddess of sex who promises to meet every human need. For a moment she seems to become reproduction itself.

The miracle of reproduction. Simulating a life. Writing a biography. Mailer himself gives headbirth to Marilyn, opens up and authors her. But another story lurks beneath this reproduction, for in the next line of the text Mailer writes of "that belly which was never to have a child."[33] The reader of *Marilyn* is thrown back on the impossibilities of reproduction, of creating a self out of nothingness: the womb is barren; it gives way to nothing but stillbirths, abortions, and miscarriages. Her reproduction is symbolically present but materially absent; it is only possible as and in simulation. The failure of biography to reproduce life.

30. Henry Adams, *The Education of Henry Adams* (Boston: Houghton Mifflin Co., 1973), 1070.
31. Mailer, *Marilyn,* 16.
32. Ibid., 16.
33. Ibid., 11.

"Go fuck yourself." Though barren, Marilyn is capable of resurrection via Mailer's text and Schiller's photography. The two men join to produce *Marilyn*. Mailer describes the partnership in this way: "Let us leave it to say that we have two chronologies here, one in photography, another in words. If successful, they will come together in the shape of an elusive search for that most mercurial charm—the identity of a lovely if seldom simple woman."[34]

The two chronologies conjure up "the silver witch of us all." Mailer writes in his introduction: "Let us hasten, then, to the story of her life. Magic is worked by the working."[35] Indeed, a brand of magic was worked in *Marilyn*, as the simulations of life forged by Mailer and Schiller set the eternal image of Marilyn side by side with the story of the life she lived. She is biography and photography—the silver of the photograph and the phosphorescence of the flashbulb.[36] "For Marilyn, as soon as one tries to classify her too neatly, goes to phosphorescence and dust."[37] And so rather than return her to dust, the chronologies allow contradictory Marilyns to live in the text.

Mailer asserts that his biographical remembering of Marilyn actually embodies greater degrees of truth by incorporating as many of Marilyn's different "lives" as possible. He refers to Arthur Miller's creation of the Roslyn Taber character for Marilyn in *Misfits* as "a lie" and not a life: "It was the half-lie that Marilyn was as lovely and vulnerable as Roslyn Taber, and that may have been all right in the beginning—a lie may be the only aesthetic structure available when working up a vehicle for a great movie star (because she can transmute the lie to magic), but Miller's problem was that he had to live in daily union with the lie, then refine it in his writing each night."[38] As opposed to Miller's *Misfits*,

34. Ibid., 20.
35. Ibid., 18.
36. Thanks to Gavin Bart for this insight.
37. Ibid., 193.
38. Ibid., 273.

Mailer's "novel biography" does not attempt to forge a single truth because Mailer lives only with the hollow left by Marilyn's presence: his
simulation is the only real subject available. Miller could not fully write
Marilyn because he knew her. Here the question of "who fucked her"
becomes Miller's undoing; Miller knew he was "living with the lie."
Mailer, confident in the seductive power of simulation, could "embrace
the lie."

Mailer's very removal from Marilyn became his license to write
Marilyn. He may know her as a written life because he never knew her
as a living person. After introducing Marilyn as one who opens up the
very problem of biography, he writes: "For an actor lives with a lie as if
it were truth. A false truth can offer more reality than the truth that was
altered."[39] Mailer's novel biography is very much "a false truth"—not
quite a lie, but a half-life, a life crafted from other biographies in
Mailer's imagination of the subject. He who is best able to imagine the
truth is best able to tell it: he who is best able to author a life need not
know the "facts" of the life lived, but rather can create a life out of "factoids"—of all the possible lives Marilyn may have lived. Mailer is his
own self-styled shaman, able to conjure up "false truths" as if they were
lives, as if they were life itself.

Thirteen years after *Marilyn*, Mailer conjured her up again in his 1986
play *Strawhead*, produced at the Actors Studio in New York. This time,
Mailer reproduced Marilyn in the body of his daughter Kate.[40]
Authorship as paternity had gone one step further, with Mailer's biological daughter acting the role of the angel of sex who has so entranced

---

39. Ibid., 248.
40. Mailer's *Strawhead* ran for two weeks at the Actors Studio in New York. See
Randall Riese and Neal Hitchens, *Unabridged Marilyn*, 504. Marilyn herself
worked at the Actors Studio in 1955 in an effort to become a serious actress and
to be taken more seriously as an actress (Ibid., 2–3). There are a number of versions of Marilyn's time at the Actor's Studio, ranging from Mailer's to
Steinem's to that of Carl E. Rollyson, Jr., in *Marilyn Monroe: A Life of the Actress* (Ann Arbor: Michigan U.M.I. Research Press, 1986).

Mailer. In the play, the subject of Marilyn's lack of children is also brought to bear; Mailer's daughter plays a despondent Marilyn complaining about all of her abortions and miscarriages. While Marilyn herself never reproduced, Mailer has now authored her as father.

Marilyn, an illegitimate child, spent much of her life longing for a father. Mailer, among other sources, reports her 1954 remark to Zolotow: "My father is Abraham Lincoln—I mean I think of Lincoln as my father. He was wise and kind and good. He is my ideal, Lincoln. I love him."[41] Consider this remark along with Mailer's final lines in *Marilyn*: "When you happen on Bobby and Jack, give the wink. And if there's a wish, pay your visit to Mr. Dickens. For he, like many another literary man, is bound to adore you, fatherless child."[42]

Abraham, Bobby, John, and Marilyn are made to constitute a representative American legacy. Two assassinated presidents and one assassinated candidate are here placed with a fatherless child/childless woman. She is the dream of democracy born somewhere between Hawthorne and Hollywood, the daughter of the schizophrenic film-cutter who dreamt of a father who was "wise and kind and good," always keeping by her bed a portrait of Abraham Lincoln. *I had a dream.* Maybe she sleeps with John F. Kennedy. *I have a dream.* In flickering incandescence she haunts us. Happy Birthday, Mr. President. The late Marilyn Monroe. *I am a dream.* We remember these representative characters. *Hold fast to dreams for if dreams die . . .*

A shaman indeed, Mailer, through the magic of making Marilyn, was conjuring America. A daughter of the republic, who died in 1962 only to be made to live again and again, chose a father of the 1860s—another decade in which the clash for an American identity led to a civil war—who could make her whole again, as he had the divided Union. Nostalgia, here, is the longing for home when there's no one waiting for you, and nowhere left to go but history.

41. Mailer, *Marilyn*, 22.
42. Ibid., 248.

Politics as Biography

> It is difficult to change that child's patterns because they feel like "home." Recognizing this compelling self of the past can help to keep us from repeating history. Otherwise, we may continue to treat ourselves—and others—as that child was once treated. At worst, such repetition is destructive. Even at best, we follow a pattern we did not choose for ourselves.[43]

In *Marilyn/Norma Jean*, Gloria Steinem tries to prevent history from repeating itself by redeeming the child Norma Jean from Marilyn the icon. Steinem writes to reveal Marilyn/Norma Jean's "real" self through the lens of the latter's gendered sociocultural experiences. These gender experiences include sexual molestation, problematic relations to body image, the role of the mother in the construction of the self, and feelings toward sexuality. Steinem wants to biographically remember Marilyn the adult by searching for Norma Jean the child. By relating Marilyn's performances to Norma Jean's unwritten history, Steinem hopes to unravel and reconstitute the layered identity of her subject. She ends the chapter "Norma Jean" with the line, "As you read and think about Marilyn, remember Norma Jean."[44] Steinem's goal is to remember both identities, particularly by reconstructing "possible" selves that Marilyn might have become had the child Norma Jean grown up to become her own woman. Though Steinem wants to remember Marilyn, she produces a divided self articulated as the two different names and stages (stagings) of the subject's life. Indeed, it is the tension between these two selves that makes Marilyn appealing as a "politicized" biographical subject—the reconstructed dream self emerging from the naturalized and unglamorous Everywoman self. Both of these selves are representative ideals. Norma Jean represents Marilyn. The biographical subject is addressed by the name of the historical-mythical "place" where the re-

43. Steinem, *Marilyn/Norma Jean*, 57.
44. Ibid., 61.

membering has relocated her. Steinem's Norma Jean resides in the real:
Marilyn as the ideal.

Steinem's project seeks to politicize the figure of Marilyn by remembering her life as the story of all the women of her generation. Her biography glides from statements about Marilyn as an individual to corresponding remarks about women as a collective in American political
culture. This education is demonstrated throughout the text, as when
Steinem remembers single mother Gladys placing the infant Norma Jean
in the Bolender home for foster care: "Now that parental kidnapping,
women without custody, impoverished single mothers, and illegitimacy
are problems that can be admitted and understood, we can only guess
how much their penalty was increased by silence, isolation, and
blame."[45] Steinem's Gladys and Norma Jean are representative of a pre-
1960s America. Norma Jean's life events are made to reflect on the family issues of the 1980s even as they serve for Steinem as expressions of
women's historical identity. Marilyn/Norma Jean's life is woman's political cultural story manifest as the history of a particular woman.

Steinem first wrote about Marilyn in an article published in the first
year of *Ms.* titled "Women Who Die Too Soon."[46] In *Marilyn/Norma
Jean,* Steinem says the response to the *Ms.* article was "like tapping an
underground river of interest." Correlating the growth of feminism with
the rise of Marilyn's popularity after her death, Steinem writes: "In fact,
the contagion of feminism that followed Monroe's death by less than a
decade may be the newest and the most powerful reason for the continuing strength of her legend. As women began to be honest in public,
and to discover that many of our experiences were more societal than individual, we also realized that we could benefit more by acting together
than by deserting each other. We were less likely to blame or be the victim, whether Marilyn or ourselves, and more likely to rescue ourselves
and each other."[47] According to this model, feminist rememberings of

45. Ibid., 48.
46. Ibid., 19.
47. Ibid., 18–19.

Marilyn may rescue her from the status of victim or accused. They perform in theory what Marilyn's analyst was unable to achieve in therapy, by resolving her childhood traumas and reintegrating her two selves. Remembering here serves a therapeutic function as it constitutes real, whole selves.

Steinem's biography seeks to reveal the "real" Marilyn. She marks the desire for the real Marilyn as she describes women and men viewing pictures of Marilyn in the 1980s and bringing a "quarter century of change and understanding" to their vision of the photographed subject: "But in these photographs, the body emphasis seems more the habit of some former self. It's her face we look at. Now that we know the end of her story, it's the real woman we hope to find—looking out of the eyes of Marilyn."[48] This real woman, this completed subject, expresses a telos found only when Marilyn is history. The search for this real self starts out at the end: we read by looking backward and observing a life story overshadowed by an untimely death. Marilyn's untimely death sends Steinem back repeatedly to the subject's childhood.

In *Marilyn/Norma Jean*, Steinem quotes at length from a 1963 "popular psychology" book written by Dr. Hugh Missildine entitled *Your Inner Child of the Past*. She describes Dr. Missildine's findings as "an analysis of adult emotional problems based on nine years as director of Children's Mental Health Center in Columbus, Ohio. Without the artificial language or gender-based theories of Freud, he simply wrote what he had concluded from observation."[49] *Your Inner Child of the Past* informs Steinem's own approach as an analyst of both Marilyn and society. She avoids "artificial language" by writing *Marilyn/Norma Jean* in what can only be called the strictly "lay" terms of popular psychology. Her book is generically related to the "self-help" books of the 70s and 80s, which were also the decades of feminism. Not unlike texts such as *The Cinderella Complex*, *Women Who Love Too Much*, and *Smart*

---

48. Ibid., 23.
49. Ibid., 57, 58, 61.

Women, Foolish Choices, Steinem's *Marilyn/Norma Jean* sets out to heal Marilyn by making the dynamics of identity-forging legible as a series of codes that reveal the costs of "gendered" identities.[50]

Self-help books generally seek to diagnose codes of behavior that reproduce "pathologies" as negative behavioral patterns. Once identified, these patterns can be monitored, modified, and eliminated. If the "self" can be correctly managed by the discursive technologies made available in the "self-help" book, then the desired end can be achieved—the self is transformed by the system. The self-help book indexes the mass-mediated circulation of psychology and psychoanalysis: the "tools" are made available to the consumer as "twelve easy steps" to recovery. Recovering the self is made possible through various technologies of retrieval, remembering, and re-making behavioral patterns in the subject's life.

Steinem's *Marilyn/Norma Jean* is a product of these technologies of recovery. By remembering disavowed events such as Norma Jean's sexual molestation, Steinem asserts the regenerative power of Marilyn's psyche in the construction of her life story. She seeks to retrieve Marilyn from contexts in which she has been falsely remembered, or remembered in such a way as to reproduce her authors rather than what Steinem counts as her "real" self. By engaging in what she might regard as a "real" remembering of Marilyn/Norma Jean, Steinem hopes to reveal the true subject underneath the sociocultural construction. She conducts a mass-mediated cultural psychoanalysis of both Marilyn and her generation as the means of healing Marilyn's case and resolving woman's place in history. In other words, this posthumously applied self-help book uses Marilyn's life(-after-death) as the model site for contemporary women's therapeutic rememberings of their whole selves.

50. Colette Dowling, *The Cinderella Complex: Women's Hidden Fear of Independence* (New York: Summit Books, 1981); Robin Norwood, *Women Who Love Too Much: When You Keep Wishing and Hoping He'll Change* (Los Angeles: J. P. Tarcher, 1985); Connell Cowan and Melvyn Kinder, *Smart Women, Foolish Choices: Finding the Right Man and Avoiding the Wrong Ones* (New York: Crown Publishers, 1985).

It is difficult to decide which comes first for Steinem—the self or the system. Focusing, among other things, on Marilyn's anger toward her father, her relationships with older paternal men, her feelings of abandonment by her mother, her mother's schizophrenia, and Marilyn's relationship to pregnancy, Steinem acts as an analyst writing a revealing case study. A fact or event initially regarded as personal is diagnosed as a social symptom—Norma Jean's molestation by an older man in a boardinghouse, for example, signals the problem of child molestation in general. A generic sort of therapeutic process—influenced in this case by Missildine—functions as the model for political cultural analysis. Remembering the inner child of the past makes possible the generation of a whole present political subject.

Steinem's *Marilyn/Norma Jean* is not exclusively focused on the past in the present: the subject is also remembered through the lens of her future. In the first chapter, "The Woman Who Will Not Die," Steinem discusses the lasting presence of Marilyn in America as evidenced in paraphernalia, Mailer's *Strawhead*, and a number of conspiracy theories concerning the Kennedys that surfaced in the 1980s. Musing on why Marilyn Monroe is still so much with us, Steinem writes, "When the past dies, there is mourning, but when the future dies our imaginations are compelled to carry it on."[51] Steinem follows this statement with a series of questions about Marilyn's identity had she lived: "Would she have become the serious actress she aspired to be? . . . Would she have had or adopted children? . . . Found support in the growing strength of women or been threatened by it?"

Steinem poses similar questions in the book's final chapter, "Who Would She Be Now?" In this conclusion devoted entirely to a "dead future" identity, Steinem imaginatively remembers a host of possible Marilyns ranging from a woman who lives on a ranch to a character actress to a woman who returns to college to complete her education. These "new" or "possible" Marilyns differ considerably from Mailer's

---

51. Steinem, *Marilyn/Norma Jean*, 13.

fictional renderings of possible selves: Steinem takes her fictions seriously. Whereas he crafts selves that Marilyn the woman might have been, Steinem writes possible biographies for the dead child Norma Jean. In each of these futures Marilyn has gone on to overcome the "pathologies" Steinem identified earlier. Steinem solves the problem of woman's identity by imagining identities her subject could have assumed had she been fully realized as a whole self. She writes: "A student, lawyer, teacher, artist, mother, grandmother, defender of animals, rancher, homemaker, sportswoman, rescuer of children—all these futures we can imagine for Norma Jean. . . . But Norma Jean remained a frightened child of the past. And Marilyn remained the unthreatening half-person that sex goddesses are supposed to be."[52] Steinem ends with a remembering of Marilyn that resurrects the phantom child as a vision for inspiring a real identity. Had the child grown up right—had Norma Jean stayed Norma Jean—she might have been one among a number of successful women.

Steinem's Marilyn Monroe will always remain a half-person, unable to integrate the child Norma Jean into her adult self. Steinem even interprets Marilyn's twelve or thirteen abortions as a sign, not of Marilyn's unwillingness to have a child, but of her desire to remain one. She writes: "None of her biographers seem to have considered the possibility that she might have needed to nurture the little lost girl inside herself first before giving birth to someone else. Only then would she have the strength and sense of self to nurture other children. But women are supposed to give birth to others, not themselves. Sadly, Marilyn believed that, too."[53]

Steinem's conception of a "whole" self reflects a political cultural desire, fully realized in the 70s and 80s, to manufacture "seamless" identities, if not the appearance of seamlessness. This real self is ultimately and ironically the fabricated self—the self that needs to be retrained, disci-

52. Ibid., 180.
53. Ibid.

plined, and managed by the self-help technologies regenerative of ideal selves. From "aerobicizing" to "dressing for success" to "having your colors done," a variety of methods and practices promise the American dream to the subject who subscribes to the proper system. This self is a unit that must be ordered and produced through management systems that contain, restrain, and discipline a potentially dangerous behavioral pattern, body shape, or ethnic identity. The series of possible Marilyns advertised at the end of Steinem's biographical remembering are similar to the candidates one would find in a career choice book such as *What Color is Your Parachute?*, since each has located her "interest" and has fully realized it in her life.[54] A woman who likes animals can become a rancher or a protector of animals, and a woman who enjoys children can become a "rescuer" of children. Steinem cataloged the components of Marilyn's identity and constructed possible selves-as-occupations that a realized, healed, or whole version of Marilyn would and probably should have become.

Ironically, the biography that set out to debunk the social construction of Marilyn's life results in the reproduction of the Liberal Individualist Identity mass-mediated in 80s political culture. This Individual is entirely responsible for its own welfare as it inhabits a world of its own design and choice—not the world that Steinem initially laments, the one that consists of "following a pattern not of our own making." The project that announced itself as a politicized reconstruction of Marilyn's history as woman concludes with a vocabulary that holds "whole selves" responsible for inhabiting worlds of their own making and capable of attaining wholeness by ascribing to the right techniques of self-production. Rather than delivering a model of self that transforms the system, Steinem promises the transformation of self through a series of systems. Steinem's "social" biography of Marilyn offers the reader "technologies of self" as a means of

---

54. Richard Nelson Bolles, *What Color is Your Parachute? A Practical Manual For Job Hunters and Career Changers* (Berkeley: Ten Speed Press, 1978).

transformation.[55] As both subject and reader realize that "she" was playing a role in some greater script, "she" can now change her role in that script. The final stage of this reconstruction features a list of enacted roles that can be traded for better parts, not a transformation of the political cultural networks that "originally" produced these scripts and roles.[56]

In a worldview that is increasingly fragmented, the "healed" self functions as a representative of stability. If the self can be (made to appear) "fixed," it can operate as a mass-mediated common ground for the whole body politic. This body politic will comprise realized selves, selves who have integrated their "phantom children of the past" with their "lifestyle choices for the future." The shifting possibilities for identity-forging and multiple identifications under postmodernism are re-solved into a whole, healed, unified self. Multiplicity is contained within the reconstruction of this coherent self: the disruptive crowd of voices is silenced, the painful experiences of the phantom selves are faced and erased. A body politic is remembered in which autonomous units of being circulate through political cultural terrains through repeated performances of self-reformation.

After *Marilyn/Norma Jean*, Steinem further develops her project with a "political self-help" book, *Revolution from Within: A Book of Self-*

55. Michel Foucault, *Technologies of Self: A Seminar with Michel Foucault*, ed. Luther H. Martin, Huck Gutman, and Patrick H. Hutton (Amherst: University of Massachusetts Press, 1988).

56. Though there may be some liberatory possibilities in the re-naming of phenomena that have been naturalized as scripted material, they would emerge only from a "naming" practice more overt than that suggested by Steinem's text. For further discussion of cultural scripting and the possibilities for rewriting gender roles, see Sharon Marcus, "Fighting Bodies, Fighting Words: A Theory and Politics of Rape Prevention," in *Feminists Theorize the Political*, ed. Judith Butler and Joan Scott (New York: Routledge, 1992), 385–403. Marcus argues that by reading rape situations as scripted exchanges, women can begin to move away from potentially passive responses to rape by acknowledging the cultural-constructedness of situations. As women name these scripting mechanisms, they expand possibilities for changing their roles in the script, or the script itself.

Esteem.[57] What is implicit in *Marilyn* becomes explicit in *Revolution from Within:* the self must heal and make itself whole if the body politic is to live with any sort of freedom, to experience a revolution from within. Steinem now provides the actual technologies of self that will effect this transformation: meditation exercises, surveys to complete, questions to answer that allow one to meet neglected childhood needs or express the hopes one has for an ideal lover. These technologies promise to aid the reader in regenerating a healed self, even if at first one must "proceed as if they believe."[58] Steinem's political vision has led her to a space of internal transformation, a conviction that changing the place of women in society first requires changing the feelings women have about themselves. If women, and men, can live with greater self-esteem, then many problems we now face will be improved or resolved.

Steinem doesn't forget Marilyn as she writes the *Revolution from Within.* In a chapter entitled "What is Self-Esteem?" she writes:

> I don't know whether Marilyn made connections between past and present or not: between her lost father and the "fathers" she kept marrying; between the invisible child she once was and her imprisonment in a very visible image that Hollywood had concocted. . . . She died before feminism made clear that women have every human possibility, and even before people like Missildine were beginning to write about the inner child. Whether or not she could have become strong enough to go back and be a parent to her own sad child of the past, we'll never know. But her life story has helped others.[59]

Mailer's civil war has been directed inside: the twelve-step revolution will take place within.

---

57. Gloria Steinem, *Revolution from Within: A Book of Self-Esteem* (Boston: Little, Brown, and Co., 1992). Interestingly, whereas the Marilyn text features a cover photo of Marilyn, *Revolution from Within* features a photo of Steinem herself. One iconic representation has been replaced with another: the self-help author features the healed self she is selling on the cover of the book. She is the healed product.
58. Ibid., 326.
59. Ibid., 38.

Marilyn's casket outside the crypt at Westwood Park Memorial Cemetery. Photo by UPI/Bettman.

In the beginning of the Marilyn Conspiracy there was a lifeless hand holding the telephone, the nude body sprawled across the bed, and the house on 12305 Helena Drive. . . . It's a conspiracy of silence that runs from the top government and law enforcement agencies to the people around Marilyn at the time of her death. The Marilyn Conspiracy still continues. Witness the repeating quashing of the demand by the Los Angeles County Board of Supervisors for a Grand Jury Inquiry, and more recently the cancellation of the 1985 ABC TV-News *20/20* report on the death of Marilyn Monroe, which its own anchorpersons considered "better than anything the media had done since Watergate."

Milo Speriglio, *The Marilyn Conspiracy*

BARBARA: I think it's because I don't threaten anybody. I don't make any big decisions, I'm trying to say this nicely so I won't hurt my own feelings. But—I mean—no Marilyn Monroe am I. I'm just not a threat to anybody. I like people. And I feel for them. Maybe more than I should that's good for me.

GEORGE: Maybe Joe DiMaggio disagrees with you.

BARBARA: What's that mean? Marilyn Monroe?

GEORGE: I think—Marilyn Monroe— maybe has the same high regard.

BARBARA: Well, that's nice.

From *Bushisms*

4 Amor Fatality

Camelot falls because of the body of a woman. Guinevere has betrayed Arthur through her liaison with Lancelot. Her subsequent rescue from death by fire brings about a war that will spell the end of the enchanted kingdom. She becomes representative of a gendered and sexualized contagion that infects the pure bodies and persons of the masculine king and his "incorruptible knight." Legend tells us that this contamination spread from the ruling bodies to the body politic. The body of Marilyn Monroe was also dangerous to a Camelot, and if we take conspiracy theories seriously, a war continues to be fought on and around her body in order to defame or maintain that enchanted order.[1]

1. This is the first plot in the cartographic mode of remembering Marilyn. It is natural, even desirable, that this plot should correspond to a legend, and that

Whether or not one chooses to accept that a battle was staged on Marilyn's living body, mass-mediated versions of it have certainly been mapped onto her remembered figure. These cartographic rememberings assert that she was not a suicide but a homicide. They argue that Marilyn's body figured in a plot to defame and contaminate the sanctified and moral persons of both President John Fitzgerald Kennedy and Attorney General Robert Kennedy. Other characters involved in the plot include underworld mobsters related to Sam Giancana and Jimmy Hoffa, intelligence agencies such as the FBI and the CIA, and a host of individuals ranging from Fidel Castro to actor Peter Lawford to Nikita Khrushchev to Marilyn's maid Eunice Murray.[2] In all of these rememberings, Marilyn's body possesses a dangerous power: she is the passageway that connects the legitimate and illegitimate orders and powers, and through which the one contaminates the other.

The threat of Marilyn as channel is linked to the mass media's own technologies of reproduction. In the iconographic mode of remembering, Marilyn, as mediatrix, relays the space of appearance through her body/image, her iconic self. As matrix, Marilyn's figure corresponds to the mass media's networks of simulation. The meshed networks of dissimulation "revealed" by conspiracies and conspiracy theories in the cartographic mode of remembering also correspond to mass-mediated forms of circulation, for the conspiratorial net is itself woven through plots and channels of information. Here the real is produced as the total of historical orders emerging from networks and conspiracies. Bodies

---

this legend should be later remembered as filmic recreation. In the cartographic mode of remembering, a cinematic consciousness surveys the vast terrain of political culture by creating a virtual map of real historical space.

2. In this chapter I mention a number of sources for conspiracy theories. The above list of conspirators particularly reflects theories posited by Milo Speriglio and Anthony Summers. These cartographic rememberings appear regularly in tabloids, on television programs, and even in comic books. The first issue of *Conspiracy Comics (Unauthorized and Proud of It),* October 1991, provides both modern realpolitik and postmodern chronopolitical maps of "the tangled web of Mafia Connections."

of knowledge and power are projected over time and space, and made to correspond to a new map of the real effected by the strictures of the plot itself.

I call the mode of remembering enacted through the mapping of conspiratorial plots and bodies "cartographic" because it seeks to bring history's hidden plots to light in the mass-mediated realm of public appearance. Conspiracy maps chart hidden plots as they unfold in the world. Such graphically rendered maps emplot the historical in a curious set of visual terms: they attempt to reproduce history's effects as a sort of evidential testimony or "big picture" capable of revealing history's "real story."[3] This real story radiates a televisionary coherence, its pieces coming together in the form of a pictured narrative or plot translated onto the television screen.[4] Cartographic rememberings further in-

3. For an arresting treatment of the category of evidence, see Luc Sante's *Evidence* (New York: Farrar and Giroux, 1992), in which Sante hauntingly illustrates the photographic summation of the historical real. Here photographs testify as traces of historical rupture and containment, allowing late-twentieth-century readers to peruse photographs of murdered bodies and crime scenes from the 1930s. The crime that was committed has now been committed to history. Yet this history is arrayed before as nothing more than so many dusty annals—filing cabinets, shabby offices, piles of photographs dissolving and unsolved in a forgotten space. The crime that rent the social fabric of the past is now the eerie reminder of an historical dislocation. All evidence is so much detritus, which we as readers of the text and our heritage must sift through as if among the remains of history itself.

4. See Milo Speriglio, *The Marilyn Conspiracy* (New York: Pocket Books, 1986), 5. He repeatedly refers to the "Marilyn Conspiracy" as a jigsaw puzzle, and states his authorial goal to be "painting a picture" of the conspiracy. Robert Slatzer, Marilyn's alleged ex-husband and a key player in the circulation of conspiracy theories around her death, employs similar language in *The Marilyn Files!* (New York: S.P.I. Books, 1992). He ends his cartographic remembering in this way: "That is the picture and this is the frame. It is almost complete now. We only need a few more pieces to the puzzle and another conspiracy of lies can finally be filed away." *The Marilyn Files!* was released as a video, a book, and a syndicated television special produced in cooperation with Producers' Video Inc.— picturing the conspiracy meant accessing the codes and channels of television, utilizing the mass-mediated modes of disseminating information. Information

dex the political cultural literacy that registers the world circulated through the channels of television.

The maps of this cartographic mode emplot the common ground of the desert of the real. They plot it out through mass-mediated networks, using the middle passage as the space where the plot is traced and revealed. Though these cartographic rememberings attempt to forge the material of the historical with the written plot, they do not finally resolve the conspiracy itself. They unfold in a simulated realm in which new conspiracies soon appear to displace, complicate, or erase the plots that came before.

In Chapter 1, I addressed the postmodern realm of appearance in relation to the s/pace of simulation, finding it as that which is always *in medias res*, distributed among citizens via the channels of mass mediation. The nation *in medias res* is situated in the media, as the media—it is always in process and located in the middle passage of the communications matrix. This matrix includes the televisual and other mass-mediated channels, including such material political cultural institutions as the supermarket tabloid, newspapers, radio, film, and the "best-seller." The postmodern citizen navigates her world in part through the figuring of the representational communities brought into being through mass-mediated networks. In this way, various political cultural literacies are circulated and legitimated. These literacies index relations to both knowledge and power in contemporary America.

These political cultural literacies are reproduced in different formats according to the various modes of mass-mediated remembering. The iconographic mode generates and translates iconic units of communication to facilitate the accelerated distribution of information, histories, and figures in a host of mass-mediated channels. The biographical mode

---

appears as representation. The Marilyn "files" take the form of documents, testimonies, photographs, chapters titled by "file number," and even calls for an expression of "public outrage," with instructions to write letters urging Hon. Michael D. Antonovich at the Los Angeles County Board of Supervisors to reopen the case.

of remembering makes the subject into the locus of political cultural memory. The citizen mediates historical consciousness and moral lessons through the persons of representative subjects. The cartographic mode of remembering, however, has as its fundamental grapheme another unit of communication. Whereas the iconographic mode employs the icon as graphie, and the biographical mode the historical subject, the cartographic mode employs the plot as its measure of communication and coherence. Whereas the iconographic mode of remembering manifests a fluency through specific, often super- or ahistorical units operative outside of any particular structure, the cartographic mode underlines the importance of structure as content itself. Whereas biographical mass mediation requires that the cultural mediator "read" history's lessons through specific persons, cartographic remembering directs the mediator to the surveillance of plots.

Remembering here is equivalent to tracking, or mapping, history's hidden plots. The conspiracy narrative traces a seemingly random series of events and weaves them into a coherent "secret plot." Conspiracy narratives fix plots as a normative standard, producing narrative structures in which the world becomes more coherent but less open to the exigencies of spontaneous human action. Conspiratorial plots allow the media and the mediator of political culture to "tell history's hidden story" as if it were a scripted production waiting to be discovered by the vigilant eye of the press and the people.[5] Power, for the political cultural mediator, amounts to a form of knowledge, a degree of familiarity with the details of the conspiracies unfolding in mass-mediated daily life. The cultural mediator is caught up in the web of surveillance. The citizen may monitor details of plots unfolding in the world around her: she becomes a collector of political cultural knowledge, the recipient and organizer of history's aftereffects.

---

5. For a discussion of cinematic scriptings of conspiracy, see James Der Derian, "The C.I.A., Hollywood, and the Sovereign Conspiracy Theories," *Queen's Quarterly* 100, no. 2 (Special Issue on Intelligence, ed. Wesley Wark): (Summer 1993): 328–47.

Mass-mediated cartographic literacies promote the acceptance of fixed plot as a normal, and possibly inevitable, historical standard. If plot itself is the structure of coherence that allows for representation to occur and makes the transfer of meaning possible, then the cartographically remembered world can be apportioned into any number of competing plots. Now everything unfolds—and history exists—according to the strictures of plot. The absence of plot is tantamount to the absence of meaning, the threat of chaos, and even the death of history—and memory —itself. Plot allows for coherence, sympathy, regularity, the association of elements, persons, and events. It operates as a literal frame of reference. The presence of plot marks the return of a world in which words have a set meaning, in which a language of belonging is possible, because there is a coherent, mapped-out, and classified terrain where events make sense and people belong. Plots allow for potentially disparate pieces of information to become convincing evidence; they fix chronologies and affix order on the disorderly; they link people in a network of associations in which every action occurs for a reason, or at least appears to.

The introduction of a representative figure such as Marilyn or John F. Kennedy into a conspiracy narrative raises the stakes of cartographic remembering. Though the narrative involves naming and identifying the hidden players in the cover-up, it also calls for a re-view of the dominant "accepted" historical order in which the deaths of Marilyn and JFK has been previously registered. Thrust into a hidden world otherwise invisible to the average citizen, the mediator is afforded access to the "behind-the-scenes" production of the historical. Yet this behind-the-scenes knowledge is legitimated only by entering into mass-mediated circulation. The hidden story becomes the public story, and public and private, past and future, are collapsed into one continuous narrative space. This narrative space is actualized as it is made subject to the mass-mediated gaze in a simulated realm of appearance. As the hidden plot is brought to (camera) light, it assumes the force of the virtual historical.

The "inside" story is established through the "outside" networks of the mass media. Remembering again performs a retrieval—what has been buried is brought to the surface through a conspiratorial chart promising the rewards of knowledge to those who follow its trackings of the real. As the mediator is rewarded with the buried treasure of historical knowledge she is made to feel privy to the insider's story, even though she is participating in a mass-mediated narrative. The cartographic remembering reinscribes power in the mass-mediated realm—a space between past and future, the place where history is made.

Multiple systems of surveillance operate both in the conspiracy narratives and the political culture at large in such a way as to circulate and envision a panoptic political cultural economy.[6] The mediator of the conspiracy tracks subjects, envisions bodies, constructs plots, and follows chronologies in order to survey history's hidden plots. Foucault describes the mechanism of power associated with surveillance in this way:

> This new mechanism of power is more dependent upon bodies and what they do than upon the Earth and its products. It is a mechanism of power which permits time and labour, rather than wealth and commodities, to be extracted from bodies. It is a type of power which is constantly exercised by means of surveillance rather than in a discontinuous manner by means of a system of levies or obligations distributed over time. It presupposes a tightly knit grid of material coercions rather than the physical existence of a sovereign. It is ultimately dependent upon the principle, which introduces a genuinely new economy of power, that one must be able simultaneously both to increase the subjected forces and to improve the force and efficacy of that which subjects them.[7]

In contemporary America, the mass media comprise a "tightly knit grid of material coercions" that introduce the mass-mediated gaze into the "new economy of power," a gaze directed toward politicians, citizens, and even history itself.[8]

6. I am drawing on Foucault's development of panopticism in *Discipline and Punish* (New York: Vintage Books, 1979).
7. Michel Foucault, *Power/Knowledge: Selected Interviews and Other Writings 1972–1977* (New York: Pantheon, 1980), 104.
8. The force and form of the mass-mediated gaze require a much more extended discussion than would be prudent at this juncture. When I say politicians are

It is important to note that the mass-mediated gaze in the cartographic mode of remembering is often fixed on bodies. Whereas
Foucault counterposes modern surveillance to the "earlier physical existence of the sovereign," these two forces actually cooperate in cartographic rememberings. Indeed, in Marilyn conspiracies at least three
bodies, two of them associated with sovereign status, are crucial to map-
pings of the gaze. The force of this gaze is iconically delivered as it em-
anates from forms peculiar to the mass-mediated realm. The three dead
bodies of the Kennedys and Marilyn also express the tension between
the body made subject to the gaze, realized through the gaze, and the
body that marks the absence of subjectivity—the corpse. The mass-
mediated gaze constitutes bodies that straddle the material and the simulated realms and are performed in the sites ("sights") of the postmodern nation *in medias res.*

We need not understand these mass-mediated systems of surveillance
as entirely disempowering or simply bent on the reproduction of docile
bodies and subjects. Baudrillard, among others, has developed an alternative version of the mass-mediated gaze and its corresponding consciousness. In "The Masses: The Implosion of the Social in the Media,"

---

subject to the effects of the mass-mediated gaze, I am gesturing toward such
events as the Iran-Contra Hearings, the Thomas/Hill Senate Judiciary Hearings, and the treatment of Gary Hart in the 1988 presidential campaign. Appearance in these instances is directly linked to a mode of political cultural surveillance in which the camera, the press, and other technological bodies work
to extract the "truth." The exercise of these "techniques of power" informs a
politics and discourse in which being subject to the gaze literally equals being
subject to a public forum.

When I mention the citizen coming before this gaze, I am thinking both of
unknown citizens who are turned into media celebrities like Donna Rice and
Anita Hill and of general mass-mediated forums such as tabloids and television
shows that focus on "real people." It is also worth noting that women often occupy markedly different places under this gaze than do their male counter-
parts—witness the examples of Rice and Hill. In each of these cases a woman
operated as the metonymic link to the private realm of sexuality and character,
even while operating as the field on which her male counterpart was figured.

he suggests that there have previously been two ways of evaluating the mass media and its effects on consciousness and political activity, one optimistic and the other pessimistic.[9] Baudrillard characterizes the optimistic vision as that of McLuhan's global village, which ultimately results in a "new transparency of information and communication." He goes on to characterize the pessimistic vision as that which he himself expressed in "Requiem for the Media," one in which the mass media operate as "speech without a response" by eliminating the reciprocity of speech and the speaker's responsibility for the spoken.[10] Baudrillard writes in "The Masses" that he "no longer interprets in the same way the forced silence of the masses in the mass media." He now interprets this silence as "an original strategy, an original response in the form of a challenge . . . that is ironic and antagonistic."[11]

Though Baudrillard suggests that his reinterpretation is "interesting if only for a change," he also makes note of a strategy that potentially undermines or complicates the role of media in political culture:

> About the media you can sustain two opposing hypotheses: they are the strategy of power, which finds in them the means of mystifying the masses and of imposing its own truth. Or else they are the strategic territory of the ruse of the masses, who exercise in them their concrete power of the refusal of truth, of the denial of reality. Now the media are nothing else than a marvelous instrument for destabilizing the real and true, all historical or political truth (there is no possible political strategy of the media, it is a contradiction in terms). And the addiction that we have for the media, the impossibility of doing without them, is a deep result of this phenomenon: it is not a result of a desire for culture, communication, and information, but of this perversion of truth and falsehood, of this destruction of meaning in the operation of the medium. The desire for a show, the desire for simulation, which is at the same time a desire for dissimulation. This is a vital reaction. It is a

9. Jean Baudrillard, "The Masses: The Implosion of the Social in the Media," in *Selected Writings*, ed. Mark Poster, trans. Jacques Mourrain (Stanford, Calif.: Stanford University Press, 1988), 207.

10. Ibid., 207.

11. Ibid., 208.

spontaneous, total resistance to the ultimatum of historical and political reason.[12]

This desire to turn history into a show is played out in cartographic re-memberings as the imposition of a narrative plot on the historical real so as to make it conform to the mass-mediated real. Plotting—and the plotting of conspiratorial plottings—could be read not simply as a mechanism of power exercised to contain and reproduce docile bodies but rather as entertainment and pleasurable dissimulation. In this view, the political cultural mediator of conspiracy narratives both receives pleasure and participates in a resistance to the "ultimatum of historical and political reason" by winding her way through these plottings of the historical. Rather than reproducing a simple brand of docility, mass-mediated conspiracy theories construct history as literal and figurative play, both ruse and drama, performed for the pleasure of the viewing masses.

The pleasure involved in the cartographic mode may be understood as an embracing of simulation. Simulation is now celebrated as the truth behind the construction of the real. In other words, if history is shown to be the product of fiction—of a plot—then the production of the historical is equivalent to the telling of lies. As these lies are retrieved and remembered in the mass-mediated realm, the stuff of history is shown to be the workings of "real" fictions. History is uncovered as the result of plot, is framed as plot. Tracing these reproduces "historical" pleasures, the pleasures of truly telling history's story. History is revealed to be the product of both truth and falsehood; telling the truth means exposing lies—in essence, retelling the lies. "The desire for a show" is consummated in the production of the historical as if it were always ready to be exposed as the product of plot, or fiction.

As events are woven together within the framework of the conspiracy narrative, a chain of causes and effects are traced back to those who engaged in the plotting—the making up—of the historical. In other

12. Ibid., 217.

words, the cartographic mode of remembering is enacted as the emplotting of what has always already occurred as plot. The conspiracy theory or narrative simply recreates a map of the original conspiracy as it was executed. This map charts out the discourse of history's plot while providing an index of the actual/material. As we read the map we are able to trace the conspiracy's movement as it once plotted, or continues to plot, the world. Cartographic rememberings seek to return the mediator to the "real" world, even as they reinscribe the real on the remembering itself. If the cartographic remembering succeeds, then the citizen cannot clearly distinguish what is the real and what is the map, the two forms will have bled into, and reconstituted, one another.

Like Borges's map of/as the empire, cartographic rememberings seek to recover the real by revealing and fixing its form. Yet this "real" remembering ultimately leaves the citizen on the terrain of the map itself, a map that has confused the material and the representational, a map that has reworked the very relation between the two. There is no guarantee that this map will direct the citizen to a region beyond the cartographic terrain, nor that it will effect any action beyond that of surveying what the remembering itself has already plotted out.

The ensuing abundance of cartographic rememberings produces a discursive space not unlike a "hall of mirrors" in which a number of histories and plots is reflected. These conspiracies may also be distorted, magnified, erased, rewritten, and manipulated in this mode. The mediator who is attempting to find the truth in history's "hidden" plots then encounters quite a few obstacles in the search for a single or unified account: the conspiracy is blown up, remade, and reimagined again and again. Part of the appeal of the cartographic mode must lie in the failure of plots to capture the real and a resulting desire to fix the plots. Once plot is displayed as a structure trying to effect, or map, the real, then it may be reproduced ad infinitum in tabloids, comic books, television shows, and pulp fiction.[13]

13. I am thinking of the previously mentioned "Marilyn Monroe: Suicide . . . or Murder," *Conspiracy Comics,* October 1991. This issue was the first in a series

A December 18, 1990, *Weekly World News* cover declares that there is "Living Proof: [of] The Affair of the Century." We learn that Marilyn and JFK's "love child" has passed a "truth detector test" confirming her identity. She has come forward because she wants to meet her father after having learned from a *Weekly World News* story that he is alive, but crippled, in Poland. The forgotten progeny writes an open letter to her father begging him to come home. If this daughter may be reunited with her father, if she may find resolution by knowing the answers about her heritage, then perhaps that generation to which she belongs may

---

devoted exclusively to answering the question "What are the truths behind the lies?" about events such as the John F. Kennedy and Martin Luther King, Jr., assassinations. The creators of *Conspiracy Comics* state their credo in the introduction to their opening issue: "We must, as a nation of free citizens, be prepared to question the actions, motivations, and words of those in power, and also be prepared to take whatever actions are needed to rid ourselves of those who would enslave us. Are there conspiracies taking place within our nation and our world aimed at domination and enslavement? Most people would answer, 'No.' Why? Because most people never question what they are told, they believe the politicians, the newspapers, and the six o'clock news even though what they hear is often blatantly distorted, or in some cases, outright lies" (inside cover). The creators go on to cite a letter from a fan that they've somehow received prior to printing their first issue, in which the fan exclaims that he has found what he's been looking for, "a comic book that questions the official perspective on history." By circulating the "real" story of Marilyn's death, the Marilyn Monroe Conspiracy, creators are "issuing a wake up call to all people who want freedom, and the responsibilities that go along with it, rather than paternalism, totalitarianism, and slavery."

The comic book is an especially appropriate forum for the circulation of conspiracy theories. Its format envisions the world in a series of "freeze-framed" pictures. The comic book is printed television. At the same time, as "lowbrow" literature, it is transgressive; it smacks of forbidden, clandestine readings under the covers at night with a flashlight. The tabloids are a version of the comics, combining the weekly news with televisionary imaging and a breezy format. Like the comics, the tabloids are chock-full of advertisements for strange gizmos and "get thin and rich quick" schemes. All of these texts are hybridized. They all employ graphia that do not extract the written inscription from other graphic forms.

also be joined with its historical legacy and find itself by knowing where it, too, has come from.[14]

In the above passage Marilyn's illegitimate daughter substitutes for the American people. Her desire to know the truth about her heritage parallels a political cultural desire to find out the truth about an American legacy—the 1960s. This truth is available when one has a story to tell that ties all of the disparate elements together, "scripting" what has already occurred as action in such a way as to reproduce the real in the form of plot. Deducing this plot, however, does not move the subject to some absolute truth or to a place beyond the plot. There is nothing in the *Weekly World News* article that suggests that knowledge of an affair between Marilyn and JFK, or of a still-living JFK, should incite the American people to action or indignation. A related story crops up within the pages of the same tabloid a few weeks later: an April 30, 1991, *Weekly World News* cover reads, "Explosive Confession Solves 30-Year Mystery! I Murdered Marilyn Monroe." The inside spread makes no mention of JFK surviving his assassination, much less having been survived by his and Marilyn's daughter. We now read that Marilyn was murdered by characters including "The Doc" and "Tony from Cleveland" at the behest of "a high-level group of advisors in the Kennedy administration." These rememberings are a form of historical knowledge that does not relate a plan of action, a model of consistency,

14. A version of the same story was written as the novel *Marilyn's Daughter* by John Rechy (New York: Carroll and Graf, 1988). Rechy's novel places "Normalyn," offspring of Kennedy and Marilyn, as a young woman who discovers on her "mother's" death that she was adopted, and that she was most likely the daughter of Marilyn Monroe. Normalyn goes on a quest to learn the true identities of her parents. She ends up in Los Angeles, where she meets a host of people who spend most of their time impersonating famous stars. She finds out that she is indeed the daughter of Marilyn and Kennedy. This novel's plot coincides with many tabloid versions of a story in which Marilyn had covered up the fact that she had a child from an affair with one of the Kennedys, and that this child is now alive—often in Texas—and is the living proof that Marilyn had an affair with either one or both of the Kennedy brothers.

or a fixed notion of "historical truth." What matters here, it seems, is that each remembered event cohere to some plot, momentarily at least. The promise of plot equals the promise of meaning, of historical coherence, of genealogy, of location: it does not equal a fixed or consistent model of truth. Of course, if we are to trust the September 11, 1990, *Sun* cover story we know that "Marilyn Monroe is Alive!" We are privy to the knowledge that "RFK faked her death, smuggled her to Australia, where she now lives the simple life of a sheep rancher's wife."[15]

The plot thickens. The cartographic mode of mass-mediated remembering is not limited to Marilyn conspiracies—other rememberings of the past, particularly of the 1960s, became common in the late 1980s and continue on into the 1990s.[16] From Oliver Stone's *JFK* to theories de-

15. *The Sun*, September 11, 1990. An excerpt from the article reads, "When they got to Australia they gave her so many mind-altering drugs and subjected her to such extensive brainwashing that within two months she totally broke down." Now, she "looks marvelous, but she still takes a lot of medication that the doctors prescribed for her. Sometimes when I joke with her to tell me all about the Kennedys and her Hollywood stories, she gets a weird look in her eyes for a moment and then just laughs. I think she remembers bits and pieces, but most of the time she doesn't know who she really is."

16. Oliver Stone's 1992 *JFK* has done much to stir mass-mediated controversy over the circumstances surrounding the death of the Camelot president. Another analysis of mass-mediated cartographic rememberings might begin with Stone's *JFK*, asking why a movie was the vehicle for this controversy, and interrogating the relations between movies, television, and other cartographic remembering. For another discussion of *JFK*, see Michael Rogin, "Body and Soul Murder: *JFK*" (Paper delivered at the University of California at Santa Cruz, May 1992). A January 21, 1992, *Nightline* also focused on *JFK*, bringing in as one "expert" none other than Marilyn Conspiracy theorist and master investigative journalist Anthony Summers, along with a member of the Warren Commission. A major news program, itself a force of mass-mediated history in contemporary America, was using as its historical referent a controversial remembering of history played out in the movies. Now the plot forwarded as a movie must be responded to and taken seriously on the news. I raise this issue to underscore the increasing prevalence of the cartographic mode of remembering in the mass-mediated economy. Other examples include a Fox television special, aired on January 22, 1992 (the night after *Nightline*'s "coverage"

claring that Elvis lives, the conspiracy and its corresponding plot structure enact coherence in the postmodern realm of appearance. These forms of knowledge reflect a cultural literacy in which plotting the historical has become a normative means of charting and navigating the "real," as well as turning the historical into the stuff of simulation. This political cultural literacy is directly linked to both the prevalence of the televisual in daily life and the greater networks of the mass-mediated economy as it circulates virtual histories in the postmodern nation.[17]

Each plot is authorized by the amount of mass-mediated attention it receives. At the same time, the prevalence of cartographic rememberings authorizes the growth of this mode of organizing knowledge and history. This mode of knowing, like Mailer's *Marilyn*, appears to be able to "live with the truth as if it were a lie," and treat a lie as if it were the truth. Indeed, splitting the real into the stuff of truth and fiction makes

of *JFK*), called "The Elvis Conspiracy," in which host Bill Bixby spent two hours trying to track down witnesses who had sighted Elvis while also bringing in a series of experts—handwriting analysts, an old Elvis manager, and others—to confirm or negate suspicions of a conspiracy that has kept Elvis alive but hidden from the American public.

17. To discuss the relations between knowledge(s) and power(s) in this mass-mediated economy, it is necessary to insist that a traditional model of power—in which some have it and others don't—does not suffice. In Chapter 2, I argue that a simple distinction between those popular cultural practices that are resistant and empowering and those that are "massifying," hegemonic, and stultifying to political action does not aptly describe the possibilities of association, meaning, and identification in the iconographic mode or the world it produces, let alone the world to which it corresponds. Similarly, in the biographical mode of remembering in Chapter 3, I did not choose to privilege the personal over the political, or the public over the private, but rather considered some of the complicated relations between the two when the biographical becomes a dominant form of organizing and relaying meanings, events, phenomena, and issues in the postmodern state. In examining the cartographic mode here, it is once again necessary to assert that this discussion does not seek to finally resolve the issue of whether mass-mediated conspiracy theories are empowering or disempowering, but rather to examine the relations between mass mediation, representation, action, history, and material political culture expressed through this mode of remembering.

little sense in the cartographic cultural landscape. On the one hand, the conspiracy theory searches for the truth. On the other, many truths are repeatedly shown to be the products of fictions, plots, and lies. As simulation is less and less foreign to the late-twentieth-century political cultural mediator, more cartographic rememberings emerge and receive attention in the mainstream press.[18]

When Marilyn Monroe died in 1962, there appeared in the mainstream press limited speculation as to the cause of her premature end— she was generally understood to have committed suicide.[19] In 1966 and again in 1968, books questioned this version of Marilyn's death, but they did not receive wide or lasting national attention, nor did their theories of cover-up seep into the mass-mediated cultural imagination.[20] With the publication of Mailer's *Marilyn* in 1973, there began a more insistent

18. Recent works have continued to focus on conspiracy theories. In *Mortal Error,* investigative journalist Bonar Menninger posits that JFK was assassinated accidentally by one of his own secret servicemen, who was startled by the sound of gunshots (St. Martin's Press, 1992). The assassination of JFK has also received attention in such recent articles as "Did the Mob Kill JFK?" *Newsweek,* January 27, 1992, and "Taking a Darker View," *Time,* January 13, 1992.

The Iran-Contra Affair also continues to receive media attention. Recent works on the subject include Samuel Segev, *The Iranian Triangle: The Untold Story of Israel's Role in the Iran-Contra Affair,* trans. Haim Watzman (New York: Free Press, 1988), and Theodore Draper, *A Very Thin Line: The Iran-Contra Affairs* (New York: Hill and Wang, 1991). *The National Review* devoted the cover of its May 14, 1992, issue to the article, "How They Deceived the President," by C. W. Weinberger.

19. In the weeks following Marilyn's death on August 4, 1962, a number of reports appeared in the media that focused on the special investigation team assembled to reconstruct her death. For example, the *New York Times* ran articles such as "Task Force Reports on Death" and "Friends Comment on Death" in its August 6, 1962 issue. On August 14, 1962, the *Times* ran another article, this one headlined "Death Believed to Be a Factor in Wave of NYC Suicides."

20. Charles Hamblett, *Who Killed Marilyn Monroe?* (London: Leslie Frewin Publishers, 1966), examined the circumstances of Marilyn's death. James A. Hudson wrote *The Mysterious Death of Marilyn Monroe* (New York: Voilant Books, 1968) on those circumstances. Neither book received wide press attention, nor were they readily available for mass purchase.

"public" questioning of the circumstances surrounding Marilyn's death.[21] This speculation increased in the 1980s, with the 1982 investigation of her death by the Los Angeles district attorney, with the 1985 publication of *Goddess: The Secret Lives of Marilyn Monroe*, and with the suppression in that same year of a *20/20* report focusing on Marilyn's death and her relationship with the Kennedys.[22] The focus on Marilyn's death as a possible homicide was sustained by the 1986 publication of *The Marilyn Conspiracy*, Steinem's 1986 *Marilyn/Norma Jean,* and the discussion of Marilyn's death in tabloid pages and on television talk shows.[23] By the end of the 80s, Marilyn's death had been repeatedly

21. Mailer, *Marilyn.* Mailer's book received a good deal of press coverage, including a July 16, 1973, *Time* cover featuring a simulated image of Marilyn placing her hands on Mailer's head with the caption "Monroe meets Mailer." There was also a *60 Minutes* segment entitled "Mailer, Monroe, and the Fast Buck."

22. The 1982 Los Angeles district attorney investigation of Marilyn's 1962 death is discussed in Thomas Noguchi with Joseph Dimona, *Coroner* (New York: Simon and Schuster, 1983), 54–56, 81–86. Noguchi states that he was required to testify in a hearing concerning the possibility that Marilyn had been murdered. He concludes, "on the basis of the autopsy I would call Monroe's suicide 'very probable'" (86). Noguchi's discussion includes a direct response to Mailer and alleged ex-husband Robert Slatzer's conspiracy/cover-up theories. He states that Marilyn's death has been the subject of rumors for an extended period of time, and that these very rumors helped to effect a "suicide panel" after her death (73). Noguchi believes that the findings of the suicide panel could have helped to dispel public rumors except that "the people questioned by the panel were promised confidentiality in order to encourage them to speak openly of intimate matters" (73). Though Noguchi repeatedly states that he considers Marilyn's death a suicide, he also admits that "there are many disturbing questions that have remained unanswered" (60).

   The *20/20* report, originally slated to air September 26, was cut down from twenty-six minutes to thirteen and postponed until October 3, and then was killed shortly before air time: reporter Sylvia Chase received "the news" in her dressing room while preparing to go on. A variety of American news media have chronicled the *20/20* controversy; I am drawing from the account in *People*, October 21, 1985.

23. Though Steinem does not go so far as to claim a conspiracy, she holds that some sort of cover-up was effected to protect President Kennedy. See Gloria Steinem, *Marilyn/Norma Jean* (New York: Henry Holt and Co., 1986), 119–35.

linked to conspiracy theories and cover-up stories in major channels of mass mediation. Some claimed that her death was indeed a homicide; others that it was performed to protect the reputations of involved parties—particularly John and Bobby Kennedy—who could have been damaged through an association with the events that transpired on the night of August 4, 1962.

Marilyn conspiracies reverberate through various channels of the mass-communications matrix. A December 6, 1988, *Globe* headline read "HOW KENNEDYS HAD MARILYN MURDERED." The tabloid article used Detective Milo Speriglio, author of *The Marilyn Conspiracy*, as its primary source. The *Globe* article features pictures of Marilyn, Fidel Castro, Giancana, and the Kennedys, along with "Private eye Milo Speriglio." Speriglio himself has now become a player in cartographic remembering, as the story of his investigation of Marilyn's death over the past fifteen years has become part of the story of the conspiracy itself. The article tells us that Speriglio will soon make a film, *Crypt 33: The Final Chapter,* in which all of the secrets of Marilyn's end will be revealed. The tabloid article sends us to the future film, and Speriglio's work, as other sources that authorize the Marilyn conspiracy.

Speriglio refers to other mass-mediated channels as sources of information and authorization of his own work. In the final pages of *The Marilyn Conspiracy,* he informs the reader that the Marilyn *20/20* documentary was pulled at the last minute because it contained an interview with maid Eunice Murray in which she reversed all previous interview positions by claiming that Robert Kennedy had indeed been at Marilyn's Brentwood home on the day she died.[24] He is pleased that the *20/20* documentary, to which he acted as an advisor, corroborated his investigative findings "almost one hundred percent." The channels for circulating cartographic rememberings cross-correlate, and thus the conspiracy becomes increasingly real, or legitimate, as it achieves greater circulation in the mass media. The entry of the hidden conspiracy into

24. Speriglio, *Marilyn Conspiracy,* 214–15.

the "public" mass-mediated realm marks the transvaluation of the distinction between the public and private. This transvaluation informs the simulated space of the mass-mediated realm of appearance. If a hidden conspiracy circulates in public it will in turn shade the private with the possibility of its entry into the mass-mediated realm.

In the *Globe* article, Speriglio speculates that Marilyn was murdered because she was "going to call a press conference to blow the lid off the whole damn thing."[25] Marilyn is also depicted as turning to the mass-communications matrix to authenticate her knowledge and story. The article claims that in her press conference Marilyn planned to reveal relations between herself and Robert Kennedy, as well as "secrets Bobby had confided to her, like the plot to kill Castro, and the schemes to put the union boss Jimmy Hoffa behind bars." The tabloid reader is informed that Marilyn was murdered because "she was set to blow the whistle on a scandal that would have brought down the White House." Now, after her death, this battle is waged by "private eyes" for public view, even as the gaze of the media turned at Marilyn is directed toward those who become involved in "solving the mystery of the Marilyn conspiracy."[26]

25. Peter Rigby in the *Globe,* December 6, 1988. The same theme is discussed in Speriglio, *Marilyn Conspiracy,* particularly in "The Diary" (35–48). Speriglio stresses that Marilyn kept notes of her conversations with Robert Kennedy, and that these notes detailed both their affair and his connections with the underworld.

26. Speriglio, for example, says he was consultant to the 1985 *20/20* documentary and is often cited in tabloid references to Marilyn's death; Speriglio, *Marilyn Conspiracy,* 213–16. He was also involved in the Los Angeles investigation. He writes: "I would mount the rostrum at the Greater Los Angeles Press Club and startle the packed house with the announcement: 'Marilyn Monroe was murdered. . . .' " The private eye may enter the public realm via the passageway of Marilyn's body.

Robert Slatzer has also gained entry through the figure of Marilyn. He wrote *The Life and Curious Death of Marilyn Monroe* (Los Angeles: Pinnacle Books, 1974), and served as consultant on the *20/20* segment, as well as other television programs focusing on Marilyn's death. He is repeatedly mentioned

In the case of Speriglio, it is an actual detective who leads the reader through the pieces of the puzzle of Marilyn's death, mapping the historical plot of the conspiracy:

> My name is Milo Speriglio. I am the director of Nick Harris Detectives in Los Angeles. Detectives are people who work with puzzles. For thirteen years, I've been working on a particularly intriguing puzzle. It concerns the death of Marilyn Monroe. . . . These are just a few of the pieces of the puzzle which will be put together in the following pages. Many of those "pieces" are now dead. Bobby and Jack Kennedy, their brother-in-law Peter Lawford, Jimmy Hoffa, the "king of the wiretappers," and assorted gangsters from the Las Vegas underworld—all except Lawford died a violent death or died under suspicious circumstances. . . . Other pieces of the puzzle which have helped me create the picture involve not people but documents, papers, official and unofficial, report and tapes. By the time you have finished reading this book, the picture will be complete.[27]

The complete picture is the cartographic counterpart to the conspiracy as it unfolded in the world: it is the text that promises to recover the real world. Now the real is being remembered as entertainment for the cultural mediator: by the time the reader has finished the text, she will have reconstituted the real through the simulated components of the con-

---

in Speriglio's text, and most of Speriglio's descriptions of Marilyn are derived from Slatzer. Slatzer went on to write *The Marilyn Files!* (New York: S.P.I. Books, 1992), which formed the basis for a television program of the same name. This book also derived from work Speriglio and Slatzer had done together for *The Marilyn Conspiracy*. Slatzer's book features not only the story of the conspiracy itself but also the story of his thirty-year ordeal of trying to get to the bottom of the Marilyn case. His text includes specific instructions for the reader as to how to effect some further investigation into the circumstances of Marilyn's death. The reader is reminded of Slatzer's remarks in the preface, "Now, after thirty years, we still may not have all the answers, but we do know a lot more about what really happened that fateful Saturday night of August 4, 1962 . . . as you'll now learn in this book. The spirit of Marilyn Monroe still lives—gloriously so—and I'm sure wherever she is, she's been watching this whole string of events with great interest."

27. Speriglio, *Marilyn Conspiracy,* 5–6.

spiracy. She will be able to view the big picture, even though it is re-visioned a piece at a time.

The author organizes the subject into jigsaw-puzzle-like pieces so as to be more easily remembered by the reader as a solved puzzle. This is reflected in the chapter titles of the book, which include:

> The Case
> The Diary
> The Body
> The Politics
> The Coroner

These simple titles promise to map the pieces onto their real counter-parts. As Speriglio pieces together the big picture, he reviews various episodes from Marilyn's life, as well as commentary on her character. In "The Body," he spends a good deal of time discussing the Hollywood Marilyn inhabited and repeats stories of her early sexual involvement with a number of studio executives. In "The Politics" he intersperses stories about his investigation with mention of Marilyn's relationship to DiMaggio, her interactions with her doctors, and her relations with the Strasbergs. In none of these chapters does Speriglio cite sources for this material, as if it is understood that this is part of accepted "Marilyn lore." Indeed, although the book prides itself on its foundation of evidence, it does not locate this evidence anywhere outside of its own narrative.[28]

The framework lends itself to truisms: there are no points in the text where the author attempts to challenge the context in which the conspiracy theory unfolds, while there are points at which he emphasizes

---

28. Speriglio includes no footnotes and lists no interviews, sources, or books. His primary source appears to be the memories of Marilyn's alleged ex-husband and friend, Robert Slatzer. Speriglio credits Slatzer with inspiring the book; in fact, he says that Slatzer was the one who initially requested his involvement in the case.

that he is not writing "as a judge of the morality" involved in the history he is relating. Speriglio writes of himself, "My motive in investigating Marilyn's death was not to pass a moral judgment on Bobby, Jack, Marilyn, or anyone else connected with the case."[29] The narrative functions with a limited degree of responsibility, as if a reproduction of the event, or of the narrative surrounding the event, were sufficient to encounter the meaning of the conspiracy itself, or, to see the picture emerging from the jigsaw puzzle. Though references are made to the Bay of Pigs fiasco and other markedly political matters, there is ultimately no treatment of these subjects apart from mentioning them as they appear in spaces of the narrative, especially the terrain of Marilyn's "lost red diary."[30] *The Marilyn Conspiracy* operates with what might be termed a version of photographic memory: it seeks to remember the objects, persons, and scenes it features as if they appeared before the gaze of an invisible camera. It does not, however, attempt to evaluate the character of their performances. It seeks to uncritically reproduce them.

The most charged element in the conspiracy theory is Marilyn. Speriglio portrays her, as do many conspiracy theorists, as radiating a dangerous power—an association with Marilyn's homicide threatens to corrupt those who come into contact with Marilyn's form. The danger of contamination is extended beyond her direct body to the media forms with which she is associated: a 1985 *People* magazine article on the suppressed *20/20* report of the same year quotes Roone Arledge, the

---

29. Ibid., 42
30. Marilyn's lost red diary figures prominently in the text. Its absence is a presence in the Marilyn conspiracy; it operates as the final representation not only of Marilyn but of history as well. It (with)holds the promise of knowledge and resolution if it could only be found. The diary has become an icon of itself, with recent topical news shows devoted to its discussion and speculations about its contents. Speriglio writes, "The single most important piece of evidence, which literally names her killers, will not be found in police files. The red diary is still missing" (215). An entire chapter of his book is devoted to the diary. Speriglio draws on Slatzer's memories of passages that he claims Marilyn showed or read to him in the months before she died.

ABC News chief who pulled the segment at the last minute, as calling the production a piece of "sleazy journalism."[31] Both Marilyn's body and the *20/20* piece become "sleazy" forms of public discourse. Marilyn's mediated body is marked as a cultural war zone because it stands quite literally at the dangerous intersection where the "good guys" and the "bad guys" meet: she is reported in several conspiracy narratives to have been simultaneously involved with the Kennedys and members of the underworld.[32] She operates as the mediatrix of desiring and taking America—those with access to, and power over, Marilyn struggle over the balance of power in early 1960s America. Marilyn functions as the conduit to corruption and weakness for those in legitimate power who become involved with her transgressive form. Involvement with Marilyn becomes a marker of the Kennedys' "secret" decrepitude, their hidden moral bankruptcy. As Marilyn's body comes into contact with both the legitimate and illegitimate political orders, she has the power to infect and collapse both.

Yet how does Marilyn's body operate in the destruction of this mythic American order? In what ways does the 1980s remembering of Marilyn's death reflect the contest between cultural bodies and bodies of knowledge? If the body of JFK is that of the sovereign and the body of his brother is an extension of this sovereignty, the body of Marilyn is the material manifestation of his cultural counterpart: woman and the "private" sector. Whereas the sovereign is the sanctified body of the state, woman is the chaotic and potentially blasphemous body that endangers the health of the institution and the body politic. It is also the gendered body of mass culture, capable of reproduction via simulation, and always threatening to make a spectacle of itself.[33] Indeed, Speriglio refers

31. "The Monroe Report," *People*, October 21, 1985, 38.
32. See Summers, *Goddess,* 326–47, and esp. 211–97, and Speriglio, *Marilyn Conspiracy,* 79–96, for discussions of Marilyn's simultaneous involvement with the brothers Kennedy and underworld figures such as Sam Giancana and Jimmy Hoffa.
33. For a discussion of mass culture as woman, see Chapter 2. See also Andreas Huyssen, "Mass Culture as Woman: Modernism's Other," in Tania Modleski,

to Marilyn's brain as a "gray, drugged mass," and describes her as "no longer completely rational." The gray mass that is made to signify Marilyn's brain illustrates her relationship to the masses, the "irrational forces" posed in opposition to an elite cultural order. The battle waged on and through Marilyn's body brings the mass-mediated body of woman into contact with the mass-mediated sovereign body.

This discussion can be fleshed out through Michael Rogin's discussion of the doctrine of the "king's two bodies" in *Ronald Reagan The Movie:* "The doctrine of the king's two bodies offers us a language in which confusions between person, power, office, and state become accessible. It alerts us to how chief executives found problematic their bodies mortal and the human families and dwelling places that housed them; how they sought transcendent authority and immortal identity in the White House, absorbing the body politic into themselves; how they committed massive violence against the political institutions of the fathers and the lives of the republic's sons; and how their own presidential death consummated or shattered their project."[34] Marilyn's physical involvement with the Kennedy brothers operates in conspiracy narratives as a political cultural nexus where the king's two bodies metaphorically and actually come together. Marilyn's iconic status complicates the relationship between the king's two bodies: she, too, has a transcendent and immortal iconic body coupled with a mortal and problematic human body. The Kennedys' involvement with Marilyn forms a dangerous cultural space in which the "great" icons of American political culture jeopardize the immortal, pure body of the king. To preserve the

---

ed., *Studies in Entertainment: Critical Approaches to Mass Culture* (Bloomington: Indiana University Press, 1986). Huyssen argues that the danger associated with the mob, or the masses, directly corresponds to the gendered cultural body of women: "The fear of the masses in this age of declining liberalism is always also a fear of woman, a fear of nature out of control, a fear of the unconscious, of sexuality, of the loss of identity and stable ego boundaries in the mass" (196).

34. Michael Rogin, *Ronald Reagan The Movie: And Other Episodes in American Political Demonology* (Berkeley: University of California Press, 1987), 82.

sanctity of the presidential body politic, Marilyn's threatening body must be "neutralized."

The body of JFK, as the body of the sovereign, must be maintained in its status of legitimacy and authority. This is true both materially and textually, as is revealed through the role Marilyn plays in the conspiracy narrative. Contact with Marilyn's body spells a loss of sovereignty for JFK: he is shown to be morally bankrupt through an adulterous affair with an American icon. The underworld keeps JFK under surveillance, seeking to link him to Marilyn's body, while at the same time the FBI— and a number of other formal governmental bodies—watch the president to maintain the sovereignty of his body and office. Thus, we are told that even when Marilyn and JFK are alone together they must keep the lights on as a signal to the Secret Service men outside.[35] Yet there is another motive for this surveillance: J. Edgar Hoover's desire to defame Bobby Kennedy. This impetus, combined with the efforts of the mob's "Get Bobby Squad," becomes a secondary mode of surveillance, keeping watch over that body which is associated with the sovereign by both blood and institutional position. Marilyn's body represents the danger of scandal if it is publicly linked—by whatever force—to either of the Kennedys.

It is to ward off this infection that "A deal . . . is struck, with Marilyn as the 'chip.' "[36] Speriglio writes of Marilyn's death: "The chip was expendable. Someone came in the night and gave her an injection. . . . A cover-up was directed from the highest levels in order to protect interests that converged on the barbiturate-craving body and disintegrating mind of Marilyn Monroe."[37] We are led to believe that Marilyn operated as a bodily bargaining chip in the war between the worlds of legitimate and illegitimate order. Marilyn has become the sacrificial lamb that maintains American political order, yet at the same time she is cast as a corrupt body with a decaying mind. It is as if she is already playing

35. Summers, *Goddess*, 224.
36. Speriglio, *Marilyn Conspiracy*, 95.
37. Ibid., 95.

the role of both the corpse and the *corpus mysticum* in this cultural equation. She must be killed as body and resurrected as mythos if she is to complete her assigned role in this conspiracy.

Milo Speriglio writes of Marilyn's death as the work of someone who understood "the importance of neutralizing Marilyn." He contends that Robert Kennedy's adversaries used "the [dying] body of Marilyn Monroe as their weapon to entrap and lure him."[38] Marilyn's body is marked with a dangerous political agency, and "legitimate" bodies coming into direct contact with Marilyn's body are in danger of decaying in the sight of the American public. She carries an iconic charge that marks her body as a site for waging political and moral battles. The possibility of political contamination through contact with her body is linked also to surveillance. Agents of the underworld, the sphere hidden from the public gaze, may themselves use Marilyn's body as a site for tracking the president's body politic.

The bodies in this conspiracy narrative have power as both material and symbolic forces. The "underside" of the narrative is made up of those occupying the "underworld": Sam Giancana, mob boss extraordinaire, Jimmy Hoffa, and a series of associates that include Frank Sinatra. Speriglio contends that it is in response to RFK's "Get Hoffa Squad" that the "mob" effects a "Get Bobby Squad."[39] Marilyn becomes the tramp through whom Bobby is "to be had"; by threatening to implicate him in her death, the mob can use her death as a stranglehold to silence Bobby, thus giving them power over the legitimate sovereign body.[40] Conversely, Bobby must separate himself thoroughly and finally from Marilyn's body if he is to assure his own legitimacy. Association with Marilyn means running the risk of contracting a political infection that will subvert his (and possibly his brother's) sovereign body.

38. Ibid., 211.
39. Ibid.
40. Access to Marilyn's body means access to the sovereign body, or to an extension of that body. Marilyn becomes the focal point on which a battle between the legitimate and illegitimate political forces can be waged.

Marilyn Monroe's body, then, brings the chaotic threat of the margins—the underworld, Hollywood, the sleaze, and the uncontained feminine—to the American political center through the president's centralized body. Her body also becomes a point of access to the political center, a gateway to the president and the attorney general. Not only does she herself use her body as a way to enter the American political cultural center, but her body becomes a means for "undesirable" others to influence central powers and bodies. Speriglio quotes an FBI report as reading, "Marilyn Monroe, the actress, first had an affair with President Kennedy, but was later passed off to his brother Robert." Later Speriglio writes: "By carrying on with Robert she seized the means to remain close to John, and close to the first family by whom, in her mind, she'd already been adopted. John remained king, so Marilyn could not become queen. She would settle for princess with Bobby."[41] In this passage, the collapse of the symbolic and material character of the king's two bodies is made explicitly sexual. Marilyn has particular credence in this form of cultural exchange; hers is a body that rests on the iconic conflation of the symbol and the material in the body of "woman."

But what is this "body of woman"? How is it companion to the king's two bodies? Whereas the material power of the king's office extends to and transforms his mortal body, the "real" body of Marilyn is discredited by Speriglio: "Marilyn was not real, her sex image was not real, and her body was not real. It was an extraordinary dwelling from which she lived apart."[42]

Nevertheless, it is the unreal body and person of Marilyn Monroe that indexes the nostalgia for the lost order. The death of the physical body opens Marilyn up as a passageway to history and to a form of tabloidized immortality. Now Marilyn is reborn as simulation: she dies as material body and is resurrected as symbolic intersection. The culturally unstable

41. Speriglio, *Marilyn Conspiracy,* 45.
42. Ibid., 75.

body of the 1962 Marilyn, threatening to bring about the end of Camelot, becomes the 1980s mediatrix from which a cultural resurgence emerges. The new Marilyn, the goddess reborn, is portrayed as an innocent victim caught in the middle of dangerous political crossfire.[43]

But even this reborn victim is reconfigured in ongoing rememberings. A September 29, 1992, *Weekly World News* cover story featuring a photo of Marilyn standing next to Nikita Khrushchev reveals "from top-secret Kremlin files!" that "Marilyn Monroe was a Russian Spy!" The editor's note preceding the article informs the reader: "Secret Russian spy files have been turning up in Washington since the collapse of the Soviet Union and its sinister KGB spy agency in 1991. *Weekly World News* will continue to publish the contents of these files as they are released to us by intelligence sources. This week: the truth about Marilyn Monroe." The truth about Marilyn turns out to be that "beyond a shadow of a doubt" she was "a communist agent who spied on her lovers John and Bobby Kennedy until the KGB murdered her in 1962." She is reported to have had a "phenomenal memory" and to have been a "brilliant agent with unlimited espionage potential."

The article claims that the KGB's Marilyn files are "the most explosive" seen by the CIA since the collapse of the Soviet Union. Marilyn is reported to have slept with Khrushchev, her final sexualized betrayal of the democratic body politic. We are told that Marilyn pretended to be "dumb as a post" while actually "every move she made was orchestrated by Soviet Intelligence." A CIA insider is quoted as claiming: "It almost sounds ludicrous to say this, but Marilyn Monroe should live in infamy as the most ruthless traitor this country has ever known. . . . The repercussions of this information will be felt for years. Before it's all over, we'll have to rewrite the history of post-war America, the Kennedys, and of course, Marilyn Monroe."

43. Speriglio refers to this repeatedly in his text, as does Summers. In both accounts, Marilyn is a pawn in a dangerous game being played by the Kennedys, the mob, the CIA, and the FBI.

In every death there are lessons to be learned for the living. Teaching those lessons and translating them into laws are the heart of the coroner's work. And where death stubbornly remains a mystery, we are guided by the thought expressed in a *haiku* I wrote not long ago:

> *The principle of forensic medicine*
> *There is no road to follow*
> *It is up to us to carve a new road.*

Thomas Noguchi, *Coroner*

Marilyn herself once told a reporter that she would like her epitaph to read: "Here lies Marilyn Monroe, 38-23-36."

Riese and Hitchens,
The Unabridged Marilyn

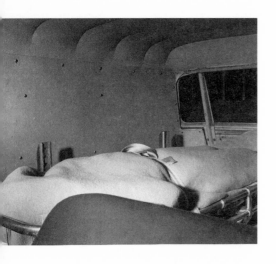

Marilyn's body arrives at the mortuary.
Photo by UPI/Bettman.

5   Corpus Mysticum

It is finished. Consummatum est. Marilyn's life is over. "Post-mortem effects, presumably."[1] And yet her dead body will be dissected again and again out of a political cultural desire that articulates itself as the drive for historical accuracy. Now Marilyn will be remembered as she is dismembered: the contents of her form will be made to reveal her history as postmodern subject. The subject of the hagiographic remembering is an historical subject whose history is over—a "dead" subject who is resurrected in death as she is remembered as image and in narrative.

1. I refer here to D. H. Lawrence's essay "Whitman," reprinted in *Studies in Classic American Literature* (New York: Penguin Books, 1977). I would like to thank William Connolley for particularly useful comments on this chapter, and especially for helping me to reconceive my conclusion.

Hagiographies generally refer to lives of the saints—they are a species of biography chronicling the tribulations suffered by the sainted or martyred. I would like to employ the term "hagiographic," with an emphasis on "hag," to mark the monstrous female who threatens the cultural order. The dead Marilyn doubles as a deified, holy, and iconic body *and* a defiled, horrific, and seamy body. Her postmortem life as mass-mediated cultural icon combines with her unsettling death—particularly as possible suicide—to form a dangerous agency circulated through her enduring presence. Hagiographic rememberings seek control over this power by exerting narrative force on Marilyn's dead form, by dismembering her even as they remember her. I am interested in two such rememberings: Thomas Noguchi's autopsy account in *Coroner*, and Anthony Summers's re-writing of it in *Goddess: The Secret Lives of Marilyn Monroe*.[2] In Noguchi's *Coroner*, the Marilyn autopsy is only one of many performed by the author. Summers's *Goddess* is a biographical study focusing on conspiracy theories around Marilyn's death; however, its final sections are devoted to the treatment and content of Marilyn's corpse. I read these postmortem rememberings of Marilyn as a species of hagiography.

These hagiographic rememberings of Marilyn evidence the relations between power and knowledge outlined by Michel Foucault. He asserts that "power produces knowledge; that power and knowledge directly imply one another; and that there is no power relation without the correlative constitution of a field of knowledge, nor any knowledge that does not presuppose and constitute at the same time power relations."[3] In evaluating power relations at a given sociocultural moment, "One

---

2. Thomas Noguchi with Joseph DiMona, *Coroner* (New York: Simon and Schuster, 1983). Anthony Summers, *Goddess: The Secret Lives of Marilyn Monroe* (New York: Macmillan Publishing Co., 1985). Summers, a "master investigative journalist," is also the author of *Conspiracy* (New York: McGraw-Hill, 1980).

3. See Michel Foucault's discussion of the enactment of power on the body of the political subject in *Discipline and Punish* (New York: Vintage Books, 1979), 27–28.

needs to study what kind of body the current society needs. . . ."[4] The "current society" reproduces the conditions of power by disciplining its subjects, creating bodies that uphold the political cultural order. The exercise of power on the body of the subject is culturally effected through codes that constantly strive to relocate the political subject within the state's order. It should be possible, then, to "read" a particular order's formations of power in its subjects, as the expectations and codes that govern "the body" illuminate the network of relations that comprise the society's grids of power and authority. A given society needs a host of bodies to constitute its codes of power and knowledge. These bodies may have interrelations that mirror Hegel's master/slave dialectic, mutually asserting and redefining each other's place in the order in a kind of affiliated opposition. They reflect the state's constitution in the construction of the political subject.

Foucault discusses the exercise of power over the body in terms of a "micro-physics" of power whose "field of validity is situated in a sense between these great functionings and the bodies themselves with their materiality and their forces." This exercise of power "cannot be localized in a particular type of institution or state apparatus."[5] A study of this power reveals its force as strategy, not property; that is, it exists in a "network of relations constantly in tension," not as a "privilege one might possess." In short, Foucault argues that the exercise of power over the body is an effect of the strategic positions of the dominant codes of power exerting their force to imprint members of the state with their marks of power. These "micro-powers" are not univocal: they occur as a

4. See Foucault's discussion of the creation of sociopolitical bodies as the enactment of power relations on the subject in the interview "Body/Power" in Colin Gordon, ed., *Power/Knowledge: Selected Interviews and Other Writings 1972–1977* (New York: Pantheon, 1980). In this interview he admonishes us to "study the kind of body the current society needs" (58). For a treatment of this subject as it particularly relates to the construction of gendered bodies, see Sandra Bartky, "Foucault, Femininity, and the Modernization of Patriarchal Power," in *Femininity and Domination* (New York: Routledge, 1990).

5. Foucault, *Discipline and Punish*, 11.

series of social and political relations that constitute an entire political cultural realm. The citizens are implicated in the power structures of the state as they are marked and circulated in the discourse of power relations made manifest as the treatment and production of the body.

"The kind of body which the current society needs" for the exercise of power in the hagiographic mode of remembering is a dead one. The stories told about this subject are told not only after its death, but through operations of power written on the corpse itself. Mass-mediated hagiographic rememberings occur in a time and place where death itself is increasingly absented from American daily life.[6] As old people have been moved from the home into convalescent hospitals and residential care centers, and as an increasing phobia of aging bodies has flourished, death has become a very present absence in the realm of physical experience. Yet, even as the sick and dying are removed from the home and placed in the hospital, television programs regularly usher into the home both fictional and "real" representations of death. As the experience of death has been culturally marginalized, the representation of death has become increasingly common—graphically available as both entertainment and news. Through the hyper-representation of death on the one hand, and the social marginalization of the dying on the other, death is simultaneously rendered a "taboo" subject and made the object of the consumer's desire. It is therefore not surprising that there is a mass-mediated market bartering stories and images of death, and that this

6. The subject of death's increasing absence from daily American life has been discussed by a number of thinkers. I have been influenced by the work of Vivian Sobchack in "Inscribing Ethical Space: 10 Propositions on Death, Representation, and Documentary," *Quarterly Review of Film Studies* 9, no. 4 (Fall 1984): 283–300. Charles O. Jackson, ed., *Passing: The Vision of Death in America,* (Westport, Conn.: Greenwood Press, 1977), is a good collection of essays on various subjects relevant to the historical experience of death in America. Other texts addressing this theme include Jessica Mitford, *The American Way of Death* (New York: Simon and Schuster, 1963), James J. Farrell, *Inventing the American Way of Death, 1830–1920* (Philadelphia: Temple University Press, 1980), and

market eroticizes its subject in an impulse that has been called "the pornography of death."[7]

Marilyn's relationship to the pornography of death is enforced by her flamboyance as a caricature of the female in American culture. Her status as an object of spectacle helps to initiate her transformation from object of sexual desire to desired corpse. In "Female Grotesques: Carnival and Theory," Mary Russo discusses the extent to which women are told not to "make spectacles of themselves" so as to avoid becoming a sort of

---

Elizabeth Kübler-Ross, *On Death and Dying* (New York: Macmillan Publishing Co., 1969).

Walter Benjamin writes in "The Storyteller," published in Hannah Arendt, ed., *Illuminations* (New York: Schocken Books, 1968):

> The thought of death has declined in omnipresence and vividness. In its last stages this process is accelerated. And in the course of the nineteenth century bourgeois society has, by means of hygienic and social, private and public institutions, realized a secondary effect which may have been its subconscious main purpose: to make it possible for people to avoid the sight of the dying. Dying was once a public process in the life of the individual and a most exemplary one; think of the medieval pictures in which the deathbed has turned into a throne toward which the people press through the wide-open doors of the death house. There used to be no house, hardly a room, in which someone had not died. . . . Today people live in rooms that have never been touched by death, dry dwellers of eternity, and when their end approaches they are stowed away in sanatoria or hospitals by their heirs (94).

7. The pornography of death was first delineated by Geoffrey Gorer, "The Pornography of Death," in Edwin S. Schneidman, ed., *Death: Current Perspectives* (Palo Alto, Calif.: Mayfield Publishing Co., 1976). Since the original 1955 printing of his article, the term has been used by a number of theorists dealing with the construction of death in Western Society. Gorer writes: "Natural death among the younger members of the population became much more uncommon than it had been in earlier periods, so that a death in the family, save in the fullness of time, became a relatively uncommon incident in home life; and simultaneously, violent death increased in a manner unparalleled in human history. . . . While natural death becomes more and more smudged in prudery, violent death has played an ever-growing part in the fantasies offered to mass audiences—detective stories, thrillers, westerns, war stories, spy stories, science fiction, and eventually horror comics."

female grotesque.[8] "Being a spectacle" is for women associated with boundary-crossing, vulnerability, potential humiliation, and public shame. Russo extends this argument to include types of bodies and "beings" for women in culture, juxtaposing the space of the spectacle with that of the contained cultural place for women. She uses Bakhtin's reading of "the grotesque body" verses "the classical body" to make her argument: "The grotesque body is the open, protruding, extended, secreting body, the body of becoming, process, and change. The grotesque body is opposed to the classical body, which is monumental, static, closed, and sleek, corresponding to the aspirations of bourgeois individualism; the grotesque body is connected to the rest of the world."[9]

The body of the female who "makes a spectacle of herself" functions as the grotesque body, whereas the classical female body specifically resists this dangerous and charged identity.

Marilyn's body is neither strictly grotesque nor firmly classical. As with many other oxymoronic facets of her cultural identity and production, Marilyn is the "beautiful grotesque." She constantly risks making a spectacle of herself even while she functions as the image of female beauty. By moving between these two places for female bodies in mass-mediated culture, Marilyn parodies and embodies the feminine. She stands for all women and no woman in this equation; her exaggerated femininity performs the female as the constructed, the spectacular, and the generic. (Marilyn is, for example, synonymous with the cultural stereotype of the blonde.) Her burlesque embodiment of femininity strains at the seams of her status as icon of sexuality, desire, and "woman." When the corpse of Marilyn emerges as one of the last in her series of grotesque and classical bodies, it serves as a foil to other incarnations of Monroe as the sleek and closed body of woman—frozen in time, this last representation lives forever as an image of death.

8. Mary Russo, "Female Grotesques: Carnival and Theory," in Teresa De Lauretis, ed., *Feminist Studies/Critical Studies* (Bloomington: Indiana University Press, 1986).
9. Ibid., 221.

The ongoing one-"man" performance piece *Dead Marilyn* enacts a parodic remembering of Marilyn's corpse as beautiful grotesque. Artist Peter Stack physically and textually deconstructs—or decomposes—the image and story of the dead icon. He plays the position of her corpse beautifully, belting out lyrics which stridently explore the character played by "dead" Marilyn in conspiracy theories, the historical real, and the contemporary cultural imagination. In a 1989 *Advocate* interview, Stack is quoted as saying of this performance, "I don't really consider myself a drag artist at all. I consider myself a monster."[10] Dressed as the decomposing Marilyn, Stack sings songs telling the story of Marilyn's death, while challenging the audience to rethink their relationship to "dead" Marilyn. The Roger Richman Agency threatened Stack with a lawsuit in 1989, claiming that his performances exploited and disturbed the real image of Marilyn Monroe. Deconstruction, in this case, had gone too far. The performed corpse was a renegade body that decomposed gender, history, and the glossy icon through its disturbing practice of gendered roles. Not only was Marilyn's body decaying, it was being made by a man.

In October 1994 I conducted several interviews with Stack. The Richman suit is a thing—for now—of the past, and Stack is continuing his pursuit of the icon through performances of *Dead Marilyn*. Indeed, the performance of the icon on the stage is companion to the ritualized space of the apartment where Stack lives, in which Marilyn memorabilia serve to recollect the living woman for the man who performs the role of the dead icon. It is filled with Marilyn material, including an American flag with the image of Marilyn superimposed over the stars and stripes. Stack unfolds this flag over his bathtub, or appears adorned in its folds centerstage as he screeches his exploration/celebration of Marilyn at the audience. To enter Stack's apartment is to step into a negative image of the living Marilyn, where darkness and light genuflect

10. See Kate Brandt, "Digging Up Old Friends: Peter Stack Is Dead Marilyn," *The Advocate*, February 28, 1989, 50–51.

to the "live" corpse who drapes him/herself throughout the home, which replicates the space in which the real Marilyn's body was found.

Entering Stack's home I felt myself to be entering a space both outside and inside the boundaries of real time, as I was cast in the light of a decadent realization of the memorabilia discussed in this text. My subject surrounded me: it was the sum total, more or less, of my surroundings. Stack has spent years making his home into a sort of cultural altar image of the dead star. Pictures of Marilyn appear behind the bed, on the walls, in the kitchen, all over the bathroom, in every space conceivable, serving as the white noise above which the den for the vampiric image rises. Stack stakes himself over as, and against, dead Marilyn's form. He moves through time as if he is shuffling a deck of cards, showing whatever hand pops up to his audience, as he pulls an ace out of a sleeve or a diamond off the comforter that adorns his bed.[11] His time and her time are collapsed into "our" time, as Stack moves from his story as dead Marilyn to his beliefs about her (true) end, to the reactions people have had to his manner of decomposing the icon.

Stack has kept a journal on Marilyn for years; he includes in it original writings on, and a series of conflicting images of, the dead star. He shows this book with a casual compulsiveness that draws the viewer into the text, displaying ways in which she, too, is reading Marilyn as she herself is being written. In his hagiographic remembering this living corpse is stacking the deck of memory in contemporary culture, interviewing himself as renegade picture, body, sexuality, vampire, and living simulation of dead gender roles.

Not all hagiographic rememberings of this female corpse disturb, or at least gesture to, the construction—and often subjugation—of gendered positions and bodies. In the postmortem condition Marilyn is also remembered as one of "the kind of bodies the current society needs" to perform the role of the Other. In these rememberings, of the sort ex-

---

11. "Where did that come from?" Stack asked with a blank stare. His hand opened to show a glittering object. As I reached for it, it disappeared.

pressed in part by Noguchi and Summers, the female subject is made to yield to a violent form of rhetorical dismemberment. Marilyn's hagiographic remembering—the remaking of Venus as corpse—is illuminated by an initial contrast with the violent remembering enacted on the "Hottentot Venus."[12]

Stephen Jay Gould tells the story of the Hottentot Venus in *The Flamingo's Smile.* Sarah (or Saartjie) Baartman was a servant of Dutch farmers near Capetown in the early nineteenth century. She was taken on a tour of the English provinces, and eventually to Paris, where an animal trainer exhibited her before crowds as the "Hottentot Venus." Gould stresses that Sarah Baartman was an intelligent woman who testified that she was not under restraint, that she understood "perfectly well that she had been guaranteed half the profits." Sarah Baartman died, however, before she was able to receive her share of the money. She ended up on the dissection table of Georges Cuvier, the celebrated French anatomist, who promptly dissected her buttocks and genitalia, ostensibly in a quest for scientific verification of her link with "our simian ancestors."

Gould reads Sarah Baartman as a nineteenth-century object of European fascination for two simple and sexualized reasons: her protruding buttocks, and her enlarged labia minora, both of which were taken as characteristic of her "Hottentot" ancestry. He recounts a section of Cuvier's dissection text, in which the anatomist writes: "We could verify that the protuberance of her buttocks had nothing muscular about it, but arose from a (fatty) mass of trembling and elastic consistency, situated immediately under her skin. It vibrated with all movements that the woman made."[13] The anatomist remained fascinated by the movements of the living woman even as he sought to fix her corpse

12. I am primarily focusing on the account of Stephen Jay Gould; however, others have written on this subject. Stephen Jay Gould, *The Flamingo's Smile* (New York: W. W. Norton, 1985). My account paraphrases Gould's longer version of this story, drawing at times specifically from his text.

13. Ibid., 294.

in biological history. Cuvier's dissection of Baartman attempted to re-duce the renegade body of the Hottentot Venus to the status of anatom-ical fact, remembering her forensically as he literally cut her apart and then sewed her back together. Cuvier wanted his Sarah to be apelike in order to advance theories of a Europe higher in the species hierarchy. Here the forensic remembering was effected to advance Europe's status in world history: the renegade body of the Hottentot Venus had to be dissected and shown to be nothing more than an undeveloped measure of biological determinism. Everyone not Other could be a little bit more human because Sarah Baartman could be proven to be more animal-like.

Gould's example stands in my remembering of postmortem Marilyn as a counterpoint against which to measure the cultural contours of an American Venus's corpse. One of the kinds of bodies that early-nineteenth-century European society needed to circulate a forensic mi-crophysics of power was a renegade body from another culture and place, with "enlarged" sexual parts, that could be characterized as part human and part animal and shown in a carnivalesque arena. This body was associated with spectacle, it was female, and it was sexualized. Its distinct place, both living and dead, in the reassertion of the dominant power codes may be clearly seen in Gould's retelling of the story. Sarah Baartman's body becomes one of the surfaces on which the dominant consciousness can assert a microphysics of power.[14]

14. Gould seeks to remember Sarah according to standards that contemporary American society might recognize, and tells a story in which she is a representa-tive of a people admired by ecoactivists for their hunter-gatherer lifestyles, who may be marked as more, rather than less, "anatomically developed." Gould stresses the extent to which Sarah Baartman's personality continually eludes Cu-vier's attempts at closure, so that even the anatomist remarks on her "excellent memory" and "charming hand." Gould's remembering of the Hottentot Venus allows her to triumph on a shelf above Broca's brain "decomposing in a leaky jar." In this story, "death is swallowed up in victory." Gould's remembering is ultimately a dis-membering, or rereading, of Cuvier, Broca, and the masculine Western scientific gaze.

How does the hagiographic remembering of Marilyn compare with that effected by Cuvier on the corpse of the Hottentot Venus? Marilyn does not operate in American culture as the symbol of a second, "less-evolved" culture: she is marked as American, the quintessence, in fact, of the American dream self. "The body the current society needs" as its Other, then, is a Venus whose status as the blondest of blondes—the whitest of whites?—is crucial to her later reconstruction as corpse and goddess. Playing the cultural role of the "dumb blonde," speaking in a breathy voice and offering sexual possibilities that are guilt-free, Marilyn, like Sarah Baartman, is viewed in both life and death as "vibrating" with "an elasticity of movement."[15] Yet unlike the culturally forbidden sexuality represented in the body of Sarah, Marilyn's sexuality is often discussed in terms of a seemingly and paradoxically marked simplicity, purity, and accessibility, as in Mailer's angel of sex. If sex with the Hottentot Venus threatened to be a version of cultural bestiality, sex with Marilyn seems to be a form of cultural pedophilia. Though I am certainly not suggesting that this is literally the case, I mean to emphasize the degree to which the transgressed boundaries represented by Sarah Baartman's equation with the native/animal, and by Marilyn's with the "child in the body of a woman," allow for their dismembering as dangerous Venuses.

Does the current society need—and I include in this the need to dis-member—a woman who has not the body of the native but the persona of a child? Certainly, Marilyn's "childlike vulnerability" is a common subject among those writing and speaking about her. In a 1987 article entitled "Marilyn Remembered," *Playboy* quoted "the celebrated photographer" Philippe Halsman's articulation of her appeal: "Her inferiority complex, her pathetic, almost childlike need for security are the very

---

15. The Monroe walk is famous, as is her rear end. Monroe herself, referring to the imprinting of her hands and feet in the courtyard of Grauman's Chinese Theater, remarked that she ought to sit down in the cement if she were to leave a genuinely lasting impression. For a discussion, see Randall Riese and Neal Hitchens, *The Unabridged Marilyn: Her Life from A to Z* (New York: Congdon and Weed, 1987), 189.

things that made her irresistible."[16] In the same article, Sir Laurence Olivier, her co-star in *The Prince and the Showgirl*, is quoted as saying that she was " happy as a child when being photographed."[17] Other examples that stress Marilyn's childlike qualities range from the "My Heart Belongs to Daddy" sequence in *Let's Make Love* to Steinem's assertion of the Norma Jean inside of Marilyn in *Marilyn/Norma Jean*.[18] By circulating Marilyn as a woman who has both the demeanor of innocence and vulnerability and the body of carnal sensuality, the cultural industry and imagination are able to produce representations of Monroe that afford a double permission to the consumer. But Marilyn is never a subject who allows for simple consumption. Her death compounds her desirability: if we read her as having taken her own life, she can no longer be so innocent a sexual subject. Suicide is the worst sort of rejection, as this American Venus wrests herself away from the grip of the mass-mediated and popular cultural imagination by authoring her own death. Now her death is the gash that must be sutured, the wound that the mass-mediated cultural memory—manifested as "forensic order"—wants to "sew up" and forget. Her death is at odds with everything associated with her iconic self: this happy, bubbly, childlike woman should never have taken her own life! Suddenly Marilyn must be accounted for in a far more serious manner. (The alleged affairs with the Kennedys and the possible homicide are other forms of cultural accounting that complicate the cultural consumption and circulation of Marilyn's body and story.)

Early accounts of Marilyn's death stress her unhappiness at being fired from the film *Something's Got to Give*. They explain that she was lonely and depressed, and that she had a history of depression. They go over the details of her life, trying to find the clues that might explain the

16. Hugh Hefner, "Marilyn Remembered," *Playboy,* Holiday Anniversary Issue, January 1987, 88.

17. Ibid., 214.

18. Steinem, "Who Would She Be Now," in *Marilyn/Norma Jean* (New York: Henry Holt and Co., 1986), 157–80.

death: her divorce from Miller, her failure to have children, and her difficult childhood usually top the list.[19] As her suicide strained against "normal" cultural behavior, so the culture in turn attempts to direct its "expert" authority in naming and mapping her actions post facto. The body and person of the suicide must once again be made subject to dominant cultural discourse and codes. The suicide disrupted the cultural order, and the cultural order must now contain the damage she has caused. If the mass-mediated body politic is to be made whole, this wound must be healed with a suitable rhetorical practice; mass-mediated hagiographic rememberings serve as one of the places in the realm of appearance where this closure is attempted. Though any problematic death of a public figure is a source of anxiety to its community of memory, suicide is a particularly threatening and contaminating force.

The history of suicide is fraught with attempts to contain its effects in a community, and the lore that has sprung up around suicide reflects anxiety and disorder. Suicide creates a legacy with which a community must contend: it reminds the living that the cultural order may be utterly rejected and disrupted.[20] When a member of a society kills herself, she casts a shadow of blame and doubt on the remaining members of the group. Why has this person killed herself? Who is responsible? Is the community a failure? Is life in its presence so unpleasant that one of its members would choose death over remaining in the community?[21]

19. See, for example, the front-page story of the *Los Angeles Times,* August 6, 1962, which announced Marilyn's death. Headlined "Sad Child, Unhappy Star; Help She Needed to Find Self Eluded Marilyn All Her Life," it began: "When they found Marilyn Monroe, one of her hands grasped a telephone. Perhaps she called for help. She had been calling for help all her life. Three husbands didn't help. She had carried her problems to psychiatrists. Marilyn—Hollywood's most famous blonde since Jean Harlow—was born into insecurity and never escaped it, despite the tremendous wages paid her by film studios."

20. For a particularly rich explication of this subject, see Maxine Hong Kingston, "No Name Woman," in *The Woman Warrior* (New York: Vintage International, 1975).

21. Norman L. Faberow and D. K. Reynolds conduct a very good discussion of this topic in their essay "Cultural History of Suicide," (Baltimore/London:

The threat of the individual suicide to the community may result in postmortem disciplining of the body. Ancient Greek practice called for a suicide to be buried at the crossroads so that its spirit would be confused in trying to find its way back to the community. Even vampire lore has long been associated with suicide: to prevent the corpse of a suicide from becoming a vampire, ancient Greeks cut off the suicide's hand.[22] Other cases of mutilating the corpse include instances of cutting off its head, driving a stake through its heart, and removing its organs.[23] In short, the suicide was seen as having carried the agency exercised in the taking of its own life into the afterlife: the suicide could potentially live after death as a force that preys on the energy of the living. The community, then, acted to reassert its power over the corpse in response to the insurgence the suicide had exercised in taking of her life. By mutilating the corpse, the state order reinscribed its force on the renegade body of the suicide, playing out its power over the body of the political subject in death as in life.

In *Death, Dissection, and the Destitute*, Ruth Richardson tells the story of the British 1832 Anatomy Act, considering especially the degree to which the act allowed for what would be culturally understood as a profound violation of the self and soul.[24] Tracing the relationship between the corpse and British popular culture in the early- to mid-nineteenth

---

University Park Press, 1975). Faberow stresses the extent to which the rate of suicide is in direct relationship with "variations of social controls and different emphases on the value of the individual in comparison with the state . . ." (2).

22. A. Alvarez, *The Savage God* (New York: Random House, 1970), 58. In this excellent work, Alvarez discusses a number of practices in which the corpse of the suicide, or the possible renegade body of the suicide, is punished for attempting or successfully completing suicide.

23. For an interesting discussion of this subject, see Raymond McNally, *Clutch of Vampires* (New York: Bell Publishing Co., 1984). He discusses a number of incidents in which the body of the suicide is mutilated either as a response to its "draining life from the remaining living" or to prevent it from doing so, particularly in relationship to vampire lore (14–15, 255). The text also reprints Sheridan Le Fanu's novella *Carmilla*, in which a female suicide returns as a vampire, preying on other women.

24. Ruth Richardson, *Death, Dissection, and the Destitute* (London, New York: Routledge, 1987), esp. 1–17. As the renegade body manifests an agency that is threatening to the state's structure, so the structure of the state reshapes that

century, Richardson gives accounts of the dissections of the bodies of those who defied the norms of the state, especially murderers. Eventually the destitute were included in this formulation, suffering the fate of dissection after death if they were not accounted for by the "nearest known relatives."[25] In a particularly poignant case, the body of a prostitute named Mary Ann Chapman—"Handsome Poll"—who drowned herself because she was unable to pay her rent, was made subject to dissection above the protests of her friends and coworkers. Although her peers managed to come up with enough money to pay for a proper burial, she was given over for dissection to the hospital as "an example to prevent suicide amongst unfortunate women."[26] Richardson writes of the incident: "Polly Chapman's inquest throws up several key points. It illustrates the mutual understanding of coroner, jury, and claimants, that dissection retained the retributive and castigatory qualities it had always held when it had been used against murderers. . . . A sub-text to this incident is that Polly's dissection was ordered less to benefit medicine than to punish 'unfortunate women.' The coroner's wish that his order would deter such women from suicide was a direct judgment upon female sinners of her ilk who might also seek escape from their often desperate lives."[27] Polly Chapman's case illustrates how dissection was used to reinscribe her person with the law of the state— to place her within the realm of culturally sanctioned practices and norms. At the same time, the dissection punished "Poll" by subjecting

body to reflect the legitimacy and authority of the state. This phenomenon is not dissimilar to that observed by Foucault in *Discipline and Punish,* in which power is exercised over the body of the prisoner as part of a network of "technologies of power" (131). Foucault stresses the extent to which modalities of power operate on the body of the prisoner to reassert juridical codes, institutions, and moral choices: while no one code may be "refined" from one moment of the exercise of power, the practice of power is effected to reassert dominant social and political codes on renegade bodies.

25. Ibid., see esp. 175–79. Richardson traces a series of debates among surgeons, lecturers, and members of parliament who differ over the morality and efficacy of dissecting the poor in addition to murderers and other criminals.

26. Ibid., 236.

27. Ibid., 234.

her body to a violation that she had earned by virtue of her dual renegade agency.

The narrative accounts of Marilyn's dissection similarly reassert the
authority of the culture over the body of the subject. In this case, that
authority is articulated through a sexualized discourse that seeks to contain Marilyn's action through narrative closure. By solving "the case"—
as in the cartographic mode—Marilyn's suicide is rendered a homicide,
or at the very least, an unintentional act. Her action is then viewed as
the result of the agency of someone else—someone institutionalized and
masculine. Whether implicating CIA, the mob, or one of the Kennedys,
these accounts place Marilyn's action distinctly beyond her own agency
and authority, or within a discourse that claims to author her biographical and physical person (see chap. 4). In addition to narrative dismemberment, some hagiographic rememberings move beyond the descriptions of Marilyn's death scene to presentations of the corpse itself as the
site of historical accounting and closure.

The photograph of Marilyn's corpse that appears in Summers's
Goddess signifies the entry of postmortem Marilyn into the virtual realm
of appearance. The last photograph in the third photo section of the
book, it is black and white and bears a caption assuring the reader that
the corpse of the unembalmed, predissection Marilyn was still beautiful.
The corpse in the photograph is not beautiful. It is a grotesque that
stands against a multitude of other Marilyn photos—Marilyn in *The
Seven-Year Itch* with the white dress blowing above her thighs, Marilyn
hugging a tree in the Arthur Miller years, Marilyn fighting for the
horses' lives in *The Misfits*. It is jarring. In it, she lies on a table with a
white sheet pulled up to her neck. The photo bears a police file number.

This is Roland Barthes's description of the photograph of a corpse in
Camera Lucida:

> In Photography, the presence of the thing . . . is never metaphoric; and in
> the case of animated beings, their life as well, except in the case of pho-
> tographing corpses; and even so: if the photograph then becomes horri-
> ble, it is because it certifies, so to speak, that the corpse is alive, as corpse:
> it is the living image of a dead thing. For the photograph's immobility is

somehow the result of a perverse confusion between two concepts: the Real and the Live: by attesting that the object has been real, the photograph surreptitiously induces belief that it is alive, but by shifting this reality to the past, the photograph suggests that it is already dead.[28]

The living image of a dead thing. To Barthes, photography emits simultaneous auras of life and death: life in that the photograph depicts a live or real being, death in that the photograph immediately creates a "past" in its very execution. To take a photograph is to freeze a moment as image—the image immediately sits as a reminder of the degree to which the moment is ephemeral. The photograph becomes timeless, even as it expresses a certain time: the picture of the corpse relays that time as frozen, dead—a living death for eternity.

In a microphysics of power which dictates that bodies remain as young and as whole as possible, the photograph of Marilyn's corpse signals a seemingly contradictory impulse in mass-mediated culture. Marilyn's mass-mediated body is that of the seamless icon, a body that has transcended age and death. Her corpse is the counter to the seamless body, Baudrillard's "point of deterrence," which defines the real, or the subject, by outlining the fictional, or the "object."[29] Marilyn's death at an early age kept her body from aging and decaying while she remained a public figure: unlike Elizabeth Taylor or Elvis, Marilyn did not outlive her iconic public body. The typical representations of Marilyn feature her in her prime, living always in the eternal moment expressive of her iconic self. She is not a problematic body straining against its iconic presence because she died before her presented body could contradict her mythic representational self. These circumstances conspire to forever render Marilyn as her "true" representational self: her iconic construction remains consistent with her body/image.[30]

28. Roland Barthes, *Camera Lucida* (New York: Hill and Wang, 1981), 79.
29. Jean Baudrillard, "Simulacra and Simulations," in Mark Poster, ed., *Selected Writings* (Stanford, Calif.: Stanford University Press, 1988). See also Chapter 2.
30. Although Monroe's iconic image remains relatively consistent in its youthfulness, her weight did fluctuate considerably during her life. Interestingly, there

And yet the hagiographic mode of mass-mediated remembering robs Monroe's image of its transcendent qualities by employing a universal medical language that strips Marilyn of her superstar status and places her in the position of the common corpse. This all too human body is made subject to a piece-by-piece evaluation, in which organs are made to act as the *graphie* that enable the right reader to tell the story of the subject's life, to read the subject in her historical relations and manifestations. The writer of the discourse becomes a reader of the body—the right reading is possible only with an "expert" knowledge of the body's constitution. The narrator reads the body as it has "written" itself: a bad liver may tell a tale of alcoholism, bruises may tell of battery, the contents of a stomach may mark the difference between intentional ingestion and forced injection or infusion of a fatal drug.

The body is elevated to a hyper-organic state in which its biological force is manifest as a form of life-writing that has been literally inscribed on its parts. We write ourselves as we live, through consumption. It is at death that the living of a life may be read in the body. Life is constituted as the narrative told by the body. This is the textual body of organs, the body read through and as its organs. In the case of Marilyn, the corpse has as its corollary the seamless, full body of the superstar. This iconic body may also have been known for distinct organic attributes, but its social and cultural force was that of a totality—the most womanly of women. Now this seamless body is unraveled and reconstituted as the sum of its organic parts. It is reproduced as the body beneath the image of the superstar.

Two social and political bodies converge in the hagiographic mode of remembering Marilyn. One is the "utter body," no more than the sum of its organic parts. The other is the iconic body, the transcendent,

---

is a good deal of fascination with the body Monroe might have had had she aged, or the look she would have conveyed. In Roger G. Taylor, *Marilyn in Art* (Salem, N.H.: Salem House, 1984), Philip Hays's drawing "Marilyn at 50" features one such imagining. Tabloids and women's magazines have featured similar drawings, or photo simulations of Marilyn at various ages.

seamless body of the superstar. Does this convergence reveal the dangerous body of Marilyn in postmodern culture, indeed, the dangers of postmodernism itself? For here is a body that is somewhat material and somehow representational: it is referentially specific to a living and limited historical being, yet its postmortem resurrection reminds us of the unholy reproductions made possible through the simulated materials of mass-mediated culture. Even the dead can be made to live *in medias res.*

Coroner to the Stars: Dismembering Marilyn

Marilyn was Thomas Noguchi's introduction to monumental history: she was the first dead cultural icon he laid his hands on. After Marilyn he was to dissect the likes of Bobby Kennedy, Janis Joplin, John Belushi, and Natalie Wood. It is now possible to read about all of these dissections and more in either of his two "case" books, *Coroner* and *Coroner at Large.*[31] These books stand as monuments of a very curious sort, blending a generalized teaching of forensic method with the biographies of the "cases" and of the author himself. Body by body, Noguchi works his way through the 60s, 70s, and 80s, eventually going so far in his second book as to speculate on "forensic puzzles of the past" such as "Custer's Last Stand," and attempting to answer the question "Did Hitler Escape?"[32]

Noguchi's historical sources are questionable, if not entirely absent from his text. His account of Case #81128 often confuses and misreports details of Marilyn's life: the coroner is dismembering her history as he dissects her body. He has Marilyn meeting her first husband at the aircraft factory in 1942, when she actually met him in her neighborhood

31. Noguchi and Di Mona, *Coroner at Large* (New York: Simon and Schuster, 1985).

32. Noguchi poses these questions and more in *Coroner at Large,* in which he has an entire section entitled, "Forensic Puzzles of the Past." (178–217). As Noguchi moves forward in his writing of history as forensic puzzle, he moves from writing about bodies with which he has had some contact, or over which he has had some jurisdiction, to generalized "problematic" bodies in mass culture.

and married him in 1942.[33] He also gives her "blonde" hair in 1942 when her hair was not yet dyed.[34] He describes the period immediately before her death in this manner: "Everything else in her life had turned sour. Strapped for cash, she was forced to give up her expensive cottage at the Beverly Hills Hotel and rent a modest home in Brentwood."[35] At the time of her death, Monroe was living in Brentwood, but not in a rental: she had bought the first and last home she was to own. Yet Noguchi makes the details of Monroe's life conform to his quick and simple narration: "Everything else in her life had turned sour."

In addition to blatant misinformation, there are other quirks in Noguchi's narration of Monroe's life. He reports the details of Monroe's last day alive over a two-page section, reproducing comments that Monroe allegedly made to her housekeeper, Eunice Murray.[36] Did Noguchi interview Mrs. Murray, or did he read that Monroe said of her breakfast, "Orange juice, looks good," in a book somewhere? How does he know that Monroe asked her housekeeper if there "was any oxygen in the house"? He seems to have taken bits and pieces of the "last night"

33. Riese and Hitchens, *Unabridged Marilyn,* s.v. "The Radio Plane Company."
34. Monroe was not a full "blonde" until as late as 1946: she then underwent a series of hair color transitions from 1946 to 1953 until she became the platinum or "white-on-white" blonde that so marks her later identity and symbolic status. See ibid., 197, among many other sources, including photographs, which document Marilyn's change of hair color.
35. Noguchi, *Coroner,* 63. Noguchi's account of these rental problems is in direct conflict with a number of discussions of Monroe and the purchase of her Brentwood home—the only home she was to own in her life. For a discussion of Marilyn's purchase of the house, see Fred Lawrence Guiles, *Norma Jean* (New York: McGraw-Hill, 1969), 300–302; Summers, *Goddess,* 243–44; and Riese and Hitchens, *Unabridged Marilyn,* 65. Both Guiles and Summers state that Marilyn bought the home at the suggestion of her psychiatrist Ralph Greenson, who urged her to "put down roots" to combat a sense of being orphaned and adrift. Noguchi, however, reverses this story in his account of her life, and has her move into a rented home as the result of her life falling into decay.
36. Noguchi, *Coroner,* 64–65. All of the quotations in this paragraph are taken from these two pages.

from various books and persons, but he does not mention the sources. When he does locate a specific source, for example, an Earl Wilson *New York Post* column written "20 years later," he doesn't offer a specific date.[37] The authority the narrator employs is not accountable to the reader for the source of its knowledge. Again and again, the message is this: the authority of the narrator does not need to be established as his knowledge is general and absolute. The Marilyn lore is sufficient to the task. The narrator assumes reader familiarity with the dead icon's history, even as he takes liberties in reconstructing it for his purposes. He enacts the violence of mass-mediated remembering on her form, relying on a shared cultural knowledge coupled with the brand of amnesia that lets this general knowledge often substitute for specific detail.

Through the act of dismembering, the coroner, deconstructor of the dead body, is now able to reconstruct his subject's biography. His authority functions to make the lives and deaths of his subjects accessible, as they are situated within the corpus of his simulated history. The truth about the subject arises from the final autopsy that he performs; it is a process in which he takes apart both the subject's body and her history. At the same time, the reconstruction of the dead icon's history is Noguchi's entry into a form of mass-mediated immortality himself. As coroner/reader of the dead bodies, he takes on the fame, the mass-mediated radiance, of his dead subjects. Marilyn Monroe is his gateway to mass-mediated life.

The coroner begins his discussion of Case #81128 in 1982, as he is on his way to the "Los Angeles District Attorney's office to be interviewed about a possible murder." The murder in question is that of Marilyn Monroe, whose body he autopsied back in 1962. Noguchi tells us that he is being called in because he was the pathologist who performed Monroe's dissection, but that in 1982 he "was no longer the Chief Medical Examiner of Los Angeles. . . . [He] had been demoted, and was in the midst of [an] appeal to be reinstated."[38] Immediately, Noguchi's

---

37. Ibid., 64–65.
38. Ibid., 55.

trial and Marilyn's "trial" are juxtaposed, creating a bond between the subject and the author. Marilyn is represented as a subject who has potentially suffered an injustice under the law, and Noguchi portrays himself in a similar manner. On trial for having abused the authority of his office by leaking to the press information about the deaths of stars, the coroner believes that an attack on his authority is an attack on the very structure of freedom in a democratic society.

Noguchi elaborates this point at the end of *Coroner:* "Forensic scientists, whether they are public officials or not, are the guardians of society. Our mission is to protect life through the lessons we learn from death. It is a noble crusade, and I am happy to have played a part in its growth."[39] As the "guardian of society," the "fighting coroner" is characterized as the protector of "life." That life is a free democratic enterprise in which Noguchi understands himself to be engaged by revealing the contents of the corpses of the famous to the American public through mass-mediated channels. Most of the autopsies printed in *Coroner* are also circulated as weekly installments in the *National Enquirer.* To quell his authority is to gag the people's mouth: to silence his voice is to stop up the people's ears. Noguchi's authority as a narrator of death's history becomes couched in terms that celebrate his enterprise as the practice of democratic politics. If the coroner's goal is to "protect life through the lessons we learn from death," this coroner seems determined to use his subjects' dead bodies as surfaces on which to reconstruct moral grounds for a pure democratic life.

Though Noguchi's first and last source of authority is always his reading of the corpse, his relationship to Marilyn's body extends beyond the realm of "objective" forensic interest into that of eroticized and fetishistic fascination. When Noguchi describes his first viewing of the corpse, he is clearly awed: "The body on Table 1 was covered with a white sheet. I pulled it back slowly and stopped. For an instant I couldn't grasp the fact that I was looking at the face of the real Marilyn Monroe."[40]

39. Ibid., 251.
40. Ibid., 70.

Noguchi has confronted the sex symbol in her "pure form." He is meeting the "real" Marilyn Monroe, Marilyn the dead woman. Monroe is his first famous corpse, and his introduction to her dead body will open up the avenue for his future identity as "Coroner to the Stars." This identity will authorize Noguchi as a mass cultural historian, and will ensure a public interest in his vocation. Perhaps Noguchi is attracted both to the person of the dead star, and the place in society that she will eventually afford him. His contact with Marilyn the corpse will help move him from the anonymity of the masses to the status of celebrity. Dissecting celebrities' dead bodies will enable Noguchi to share in their fame and glory—to enter into the aura of the iconic polis. It is not surprising that his encounter with Marilyn's corpse sends him into raptures.

Noguchi seems to agree with Poe that the death of a beautiful woman is the most poetic subject imaginable.[41] He states that when asked of Marilyn's appearance in death he "could reply only with the words of the Latin poet Petrarch: 'It's folly to shrink in fear, if this is dying/For death looked lovely in her lovely face.' "[42] The beautiful corpse, however, is soon dismembered under the exacting forces of Noguchi's pen, eye, and blade. Though he initially assures the reader of Marilyn's beauty while she remains intact, death's lovely face is soon replaced by a detailed discussion of her urinary tract, bilary systems, and other bodily organs and systems. The dead Marilyn Monroe is accessible only to the coroner; he performs the only possible reading on/of her body and thereby writes her story. She has become a series of surfaces that Noguchi alone may read, an aggregate of organs to puncture, weigh, evaluate. She will be made to yield her self to him, to relinquish "the truth" piece by piece.

41. For a discussion of Poe, women, and death, see Elizabeth Bronfen, *Over Her Dead Body* (New York: Routledge, 1992). See also Shawn Rosenheim, *The King of Secret Readers and the Cryptographic Imagination* (forthcoming), for an excellent discussion of Poe as posthumous icon.
42. Noguchi, *Coroner,* 56.

As the coroner maps Monroe's life and death, he quotes from his "original" report on Marilyn's body. This report takes on the status of a separate canonical text that now operates as evidence informing the present remembering of Monroe. In the original report, it seems, are outlined the traces of the *real* dead body. By repeatedly quoting his original "writing" of Marilyn, Noguchi reinscribes her in a discursive field of power in which she is available only to him: "EXTERNAL EXAMI-NATION: The unembalmed body is that of a thirty-six-year-old, well-developed, well-nourished, Caucasian female weighing 117 pounds and measuring sixty-five and one-half inches in length. The scalp is covered with bleached blonde hair. The eyes are blue . . . a slight ecchymotic area [i.e., bruise] is noted on the left hip and left side of lower back."[43] The Marilyn figure of pinup proportions has been transformed into an unembalmed body through Noguchi's pen. Marilyn is now a race (Caucasian), a weight (117 pounds), and a length (sixty-five and one-half inches). She is a series of figures to be recorded. She is no longer even a blonde but a "scalp covered with bleached blonde hair." As each part is listed as a separate category, transforming her into a list of body traits and parts, she gains identity as a type and becomes accessible to "scientific" evaluation. The written word reenacts the actual dissection process that her unembalmed body is to undergo. She is rewritten from sex symbol status to medical statistic.

Noguchi continues with his written dissection: "The report then went on to detail my internal examination of Monroe's cardiovascular, respiratory, liver and bilary, hemic and lymphatic, endocrine, urinary, genital and digestive systems."[44] Marilyn's body has now been translated from an iconicity based on the glittering transcendence of bodily forms to a "scientific" physicality that is nothing more than an aggregate of organs. She has become a series of biological systems, capable of being weighed, penetrated, measured, studied. By transforming the "star" into

---

43. Ibid., 72.
44. Ibid., 72.

a series of "systems," a specific manifestation of biologically recurrent norms, the text has stripped Monroe of her elevated cultural status. Now she is the same as every body: every body has these systems; no body is above the definition of the system.

As Marilyn's body and history are simultaneously taken apart and re-membered, so the narrative form of *Coroner* asserts the violence and rupture of the autopsy as a model for historical discourse. The subject is rendered the sum of her parts, while the narrator emerges whole and in-tact. Whereas the body is readily shown to be nothing more than pieces, the narrative strains to be seamless.

The narrator, however, is not a single voice. The position of the nar-rator in *Coroner* is complicated by the role of Joseph DiMona, lawyer and writer, who has written the book with Noguchi. The exact nature of this writing relationship is unclear; however, DiMona is listed as a "professional" writer. In "About the Authors" we read: "Joseph DiMona began his writing career on the *Washington Post*. . . . His books include the best-selling novels *Last Man at Arlington* and *The Benedict Arnold Connection*. . . . Mr. DiMona is a lawyer and member of the bar of the District of Columbia."[45] As Noguchi's credentials lie in his role as Los Angeles county examiner and his direct proximity to most of the bodies he examines, DiMona's seem to come from his dual identity as lawyer and writer. The cluster of these three positions—lawyer, writer, coro-ner—suggests a crystallization of micropowers in the postmortem mode. Each of these vocations rests in a relationship to narrative au-thority based on reconstructing "the story" from seemingly disparate clues so as to produce effects of coherence.

The story that circulates through the postmortem historical con-sciousness of this unholy trinity is expressed in a remembering that fea-tures the narrator himself as heroic subject—the fighting coroner snatching truth from the jaws of death. Other cast members in this his-torical drama include "the state" or democracy, "the people" or the

45. Ibid., 253.

readers of the book, and the corpses of the famous. As Noguchi (de)faces each of these famous corpses and reveals their contents to "the people," he becomes both Homer and Hercules in his mythifying discursive practice. The act of narrating the dissection itself becomes heroic, as the hero/coroner faces the monster/corpse of Monroe and "tames" it via the agency of forensic discourse. Is he the hero of "the state" or "the people," some blend of the two, or an agent outside of the democratic equation who allows for the retrieval of the body politic as mass cultural corpus? Or are the heroes of this story "the people" themselves, popular culture, rebelling against the mass-mediated cultural elite, whose famous iconic bodies have now become the corpses of Everymen?

In the postmortem polis of remembrance, the democratic story is reconstituted through a public space that reveals literal and figurative "insides" ostensibly to clarify the unified historical "outside" or truth. When being is only accessible as the residual effects left behind on an organ, when the body/image of a superstar is dissected so as to make her both more "real" and democratically accessible, when the lessons we learn from death seem to point to little beyond an obsession with fame and a right to know, what have we learned? The story itself is anything but historically accurate; the moral, if any, is muddy. The narrative seems to have existed to elevate the author to an heroic status, and yet his story is nothing more than a table of contents, however graphically violent and sexualized.

I have already discussed the extent to which the greater cultural narration of Marilyn's death—in which I include Noguchi's work—attempts to resolve her dangerous and disturbing renegade presence and power. I am suggesting that her power is linked to death and disorder—that is, the presence of chaos. As the agent of chaos, Marilyn radiates a dangerous and transgressive charge; she is the woman who should never have killed herself, but did. This power is doubly frightening because it is associated with her charge as a mass-mediated cultural icon extraordinaire—the "unique" and "original" simulacrum of woman, fame, innocence, sexuality, and America. Marilyn the mediatrix is resurrected in the hagiographic mode of remembering as a democratic corpse, a body like every body, ultimately subject to the coroner's authority. He tells the final story and authors the lessons we must learn from death. But these lessons are most present in his text as an absence. The lessons we read here are not those he has authored explicitly, but rather those we may extract from the dynamic of the text itself. What have Noguchi and his text finally told us? It appears that the story has died along with the author and the subject. We are left with a body.

The Postmortem Goddess

After *Coroner,* it was difficult to imagine the form that Marilyn's hagiographic remembering would next assume, but from the flames there arose a *Goddess* who breathed new life into the corpus of Monroe's corpse. Advertised as the "only documented story of Marilyn Monroe by a master investigative journalist," *Goddess* drew on "more than six hundred interviews, her psychiatrist's private correspondence, hidden police reports, suppressed phone records," and "more."[46] Summers's book sought, in his words, "to grant this goddess a measure of reality."[47]

Summers frames "the phenomenon of Marilyn Monroe" in the following passage: "Who was the woman who turned herself into 'Marilyn Monroe?' She had a body, in truth, not so unlike other female bodies. How did she make us notice her more than any other woman, in her time, and on into the end of the century? How much of this alchemy was achieved by talent, how much in carefully chosen embraces of powerful males? What was at the hidden center of this phenomenon that was Marilyn Monroe?"[48] Summers navigates the hidden center of Marilyn's mystery by focusing primarily on her adulthood, and stressing her relationships with the Kennedys and the mob. He opts to spend very little time on Marilyn's childhood: "This book will be an investigation

46. Summers, *Goddess,* jacket copy of casebound edition.
47. Ibid., 5.
48. Ibid., 4.

of Marilyn's adult life, not of her childhood—that desolate, dislocated period has been well charted by earlier biographers."[49] A reversal of standard biographical practice takes place at the outset of his work: the death and subsequent treatment of the corpse are given more "space" in the text than the childhood. In *Goddess,* we are made to understand that Marilyn's roots are in her death. Is this his proof that Marilyn had "a body, in truth, not so unlike other female bodies"?

Summers begin the narration of his project, after a brief discussion of activities occurring at the time of Monroe's death in 1962, with the 1982 hearing—the same point Noguchi chose as the point of origin for his story. Summers writes that the investigation of Marilyn's death as a possible murder drew him into a labyrinth where he "soon realized it would be pointless to tackle the death issue without months of research."[50] Marilyn's death has become "the death issue," which may be tackled by assembling the secondary body of information taken here as the effects of Marilyn's life. The life is literally made up of this secondary body, pieced together by the master assembler, the investigative journalist. Of course, even this seemingly neutral body of information is subject to the authority of the narrator's pen and person: as Summers sorts through the pieces of the story, he decides what does and does not legitimately constitute Marilyn's "factual" body. What Summers chooses to deem part of Marilyn's factual body requires the creation of a second fantasy body, the body of Marilyn as goddess, the mass-mediated cultural icon who refuses to die. He renders the treatment of her corpse in terms that underscore its twinned status as object of desire and subject for authoritative inscription.[51]

Summers first describes Marilyn's body in this way: "By 10:30 A.M. on August 5, within six hours of the first official knowledge that Marilyn

49. Ibid., 7.
50. Ibid., 9.
51. For the dates and details of Marilyn's death and associated conspiracies and events tracked by the author, see the final one hundred and fifty pages of *Goddess.*

was dead, the most highly advertised, overpromoted body on earth lay, covered by a plastic sheet, in a long windowless room in the hall of justice. Eddy Day, the Autopsy assistant, had prepared Marilyn on Table 1, a stainless-steel slab equipped with a water hose and drainage system, and a scale for weighing human organs."[52] The star's body is written in terms that mark it simultaneously as the product of commodity relations and the subject of forensic evaluation. The iconic body of Marilyn is disparaged as "overpromoted," and will now be deconstructed with the tools of science. As these tools are inventoried in a flat, dry tone, the text reenacts the evaluative medical practice of "stripping bare" the glamorous mass-cultural body and replacing it with a body forced to emit signs in a rational and scientized discourse.

Summers evokes Noguchi in this process, noting that the coroner has become a controversial figure and stating that Noguchi was profoundly affected by the sight of Monroe's corpse. He quotes Noguchi's assistant: "Tom and I had looked at thousands of bodies, but we were both very touched. We had . . . the feeling that this young, young woman could stand up and get off the table at any minute."[53]

"This young, young woman" does not stand up, however. She is dissected in narrative as a series of graphic images and organs corresponding to those of the living icon Marilyn Monroe. The juxtaposition of the "young, young woman" and the mysterious corpse constitutes the double body beneath the hagiographic discourse: Marilyn is once more simultaneously the body who would not die and the utterly dead body. She is Everywoman and famous star—the tragic young, young death, and the corpse who jars the coroners who have looked at "thousands of bodies."

Summers reconstructs Noguchi's autopsy in his narrative, which is itself reminiscent of Noguchi's in *Coroner:* "Noguchi laboured over Marilyn for hours, his scalpel slicing into the body that had graced so

---

52. Ibid., 318.
53. Ibid.

many pinups, his surgeon's saw carving a way to remove the brain that had made millions lust and laugh."[54] The language employed in this description simultaneously sexualizes and violates the body of Marilyn. She is subject to the full power of her dissector, reduced to the status of mute statistic/object. The extent to which this status sits in obverse relation to the object that "made millions lust and laugh," and that "graced so many pinups" is played out by a physical and rhetorical violence that cuts open the desired body and removes the brain. The stress on the brain is curious but not accidental, for though it is not the likely object of lust, its removal literalizes the mind/body split being enacted as rhetorical violence to the beautiful grotesque. The brain's removal punctuates the dead Marilyn's status as utterly dead body, even while its association with "lust" asserts her sexualized position as living star and dead icon. The utterly dead body emerges as a companion to the mass icon, the body without organs. Now the body that "graced so many pinups" reappears as a corpse, a corpse without a brain.

Concluding his narration of Noguchi's autopsy, Summers writes: "When Marilyn was wheeled away, the beauty was gone. A picture retrieved from police files—the only known surviving post mortem photograph—shows a sagging, bloated face, hair hanging limp and straight over the edge of the table. The facial muscles had been severed during the removal of the brain, and the remains sluiced with water once the doctor's work was done."[55]

Marilyn the pinup queen is reduced to "a picture retrieved from police files." The once beautiful face is now "sagging, bloated"; the hair is limp, the facial muscles severed, the brain removed. Why is this graphic detail necessary, why must the resolution of Marilyn's death involve the description of her corpse, and why must this corpse sit in opposition to the glossy, sexual body of desire associated with the iconic Marilyn? Summers is dismembering, and thereby introducing, the "hag" Marilyn

54. Ibid.
55. Ibid.

Monroe. The hag replaces the beautiful, living woman by surviving as a postmortem photograph democratically numbered and labeled.

The narrative detailing of the bloated corpse is accompanied by the retrieved police photo of Case #81128. The caption reads: "Marilyn in death. The photograph, taken after autopsy, bears a police file number. The facial discoloration occurred after death, and it is the surgeon's work that caused her face to sag. Before the procedure, say those present, the lifeless Marilyn remained beautiful."[56] The image of the dead Marilyn is the image of death. Is this the image that lurked beneath the body without organs circulated in the culture? Is this the image that must be exorcised once and for all? Does the reproduction of her dead image seek to kill her off, to lay her to rest, to solve her case? Is the image the perpetuation of a form of violence on her person, an attempt to wrest away the authority she exercised as suicide? If the photo is a further writing of power relations on her very body, what knowledge does it produce? Does this knowledge lurk always beneath mass culture, a death's-head waiting to peek from behind the glossy pages of popular magazines?

Walter Benjamin, in his essay "The Storyteller," writes of the retreat of death from everyday Western life (see n. 6). Following this, he discusses the act of storytelling as it relates to death. He writes that even "the poorest wretch" has at the moment of death an "authority" in the reconstruction of his own life story—the images that bombard him resonate particularly with the life he has lived, and make him at that moment its greatest storyteller. Death, in this sense, gives birth to narrative authority.

Benjamin writes of the authority born at the moment of death: "This authority is at the very source of the story. . . . Death is the sanction of everything that the storyteller can tell. He has borrowed his authority from death."[57] It is not simply in the hagiographic mode of remember-

---

56. Ibid., 359.
57. Benjamin, *Illuminations,* 94.

ing Marilyn, but in all of her reconstructions, that her death lends an authority to the tellers of her story. Knowing the truth about the mystery of her death informs biography, song, and conspiracy theory; saying good-bye to this woman, who has been dead now for almost as many years as she lived, has become an American pastime of sorts. Benjamin writes: "A man . . . who died at thirty-five will appear to remembrance at every point in his life as a man who dies at the age of thirty-five. In other words, the statement that makes no sense for real life becomes indisputable for remembered life."[58]

Marilyn's life is read backward from her death at thirty-six; to fix the resolution of her death's story is to fix her life story. And yet, in the hagiographic mode of remembering Marilyn, the storyteller has moved beyond telling the story of her death to death's story itself—the story of the corpse and its contents, that history which is the body at death. As daily life in the present moves increasingly into the realms of representation and simulation, a familiarity with the construction of narratives that seek closure becomes fundamental to the history of the everyday. We make up stories about what has happened even as it is happening, hoping to somehow "fix" the object of narrative with an iconic nomenclature capable of reproducing—and "taming"—reality. Is there an impulse in this remembering of Marilyn not simply to tame her cultural power but to further domesticate and quantify death, to somehow resolve death and its object and thereby conquer death itself? The goddess that emerges at the end of Summers's book has done just this: she is reborn in the whole icon body form once more, in which she functions as tainted saint, electronic virgin, and virtual matrix. The hag is made beautiful.

In the final section of Summers's book, entitled "Aftermath," Marilyn's corpse is reconstituted as the body of a goddess. First the reader is made privy to the problems involved in reconstructing the body of the dead star after the coroner has done his work. Summers be-

58. Ibid., 94.

gins this section with the words Marilyn spoke to her makeup man Whitney Snyder during the filming of *Gentlemen Prefer Blondes:* "If anything happens to me promise me you'll make me up." She sealed this pact by giving a gold clip to Snyder with the inscription "While I'm Still Warm, Marilyn." Summers begins his final section with Snyder heading off to reconstruct Marilyn, bringing along the clip and a bottle of gin: "It fell to Snyder and his future wife, Marilyn's longtime wardrobe assistant Marjorie Plecher, to restore the embalmed ruin that had been Marilyn's body." Summers goes on to say: "The famous figure was gone. . . . After the surgeon's assault, the swelling breasts were no more."[59] Summers tells us that Marilyn's body was reconstructed with some cushion stuffing and plastic bags. When Snyder and Plecher were done, "She looked beautiful, like a beautiful doll."

Summers moves quickly from the final image of the corpse to a brief discussion of Marilyn's resurrection as "Everyman's Goddess"—the symbol of an age in which few are remembered and revered. He gives no long justification of her status as goddess: this is simply a shared cultural truth that he assumes, that reverberates even in the title of his book, his naming of the subject. The "beautiful doll" is positively beatific at the book's end—she is great, big, and radiant. What matter that she is also a stuffed corpse, silent, and yielding? In a few simple sentences he moves away from the stuffed, dyed corpse to the glossy iconic figure. Marilyn has been retrieved as a goddess, even while she has been disciplined, violated, and democratized. And she continues to radiate a dangerous power even as this occurs. For somehow "she" manages to survive the narrative assault, the violence of dismembering, and appear at the end of the text intact.

And so we end with Marilyn once again a kind of goddess. In the hagiographic mode of remembering this return does not require a lot of time because the corpse and the saint/Virgin/goddess are simultaneously present in the contested figure. Indeed, the position of the

59. Summers, *Goddess,* 359.

corpus mysticum requires a dead Marilyn, so that she can later be resurrected, made to live forever. After death the goddess is reborn, and when she is reborn she may be dismembered once again. This is what one does with a goddess, and now with the help of mass-mediated mechanisms we can do it in Technicolor.

And so this play between re-membering and dismembering, resurrection and dissection, is continually enacted. In this work I have sought to take the forms of this remembering seriously, to read them as reflective of cultural codes that organize the spoken world in our time. To this end I have focused on a mythico-religious political female character, exploring some of the ways she has been remembered, known, made to live again, and made to die again, on into the late twentieth century. Yet even as I have sought to take the forms of her remembering seriously, I wish to simultaneously advocate a sort of "serious irony," a strategy explored by feminist political theorist Donna Haraway.

As representative character, Marilyn is an ironic goddess to be sure, a goddess who undoes simple notions of the holy. In this ironic undoing there are possibilities for liberation and engagement, even while there remains a recognition of the limits of such transformation. I think here of Donna Haraway's discussion of irony as a strategy in political myth-building: "Irony is about contradictions that do not resolve into larger wholes, even dialectically, about the tension of holding incompatible things together because both or all are necessary and true. Irony is about humor and serious play. It is also a rhetorical strategy and a political method."[60] By taking Marilyn as a kind of goddess, I both assert her power as mass-mediated icon and point to its limits. Possibilities of power lie in her gendered equation with the media, in the ways in which her figure undoes such simple polarities as politics versus culture, the public versus the private, and that which is real versus that which is material. She offers possibilities particularly for feminist theorizations of the political, allowing for an articulation of the disciplinary tactics of

60. Donna J. Haraway, *Simians, Cyborgs, and Women: The Reinvention of Nature* (New York: Routledge, 1991), 149.

rhetorical strategies while at the same time eluding those strategies through the force of her constant reconstruction. Nevertheless, my discussion of these mass-mediated modes of remembering must constantly acknowledge their limits. As a subject of these forces of remembering, Marilyn is so often made to occupy positions of subjection, transgression, and punishment.[61] To celebrate Marilyn as a goddess without noting the many ways in which her cultural resurrections have sought to contain her would be to erase the context of her remembering. In this ironic examination of the postmodern goddess, I have sought to attend to both her possibilities as expression of a reconstituted real and her markings of the limits of such expression.

I cannot resurrect this goddess once and for all, nor do I care to. I cannot solve her, make her whole, tell you who killed her or if she killed herself. She sends me forward as I go backward, reverses my sensibilities; the ways of her inscription layer, they do not line. She is a kind of virgin mother, made to give birth to a transcendent self: she can be resurrected in a matter of seconds and made prey again the hour of her death. Icon, American dream, dangerous passageway, corpse, goddess—she appears in all of these forms and more. She radiates the stuff of history in our time, mass-mediated memory. She is bigger than life, she lives longer than death. She winks at us. She is smiling. As she walks away from us, this angel of history, we can still glimpse the living end.

Theorist as Answering Machine

> Blonde and beautiful Marilyn Monroe, a glamorous symbol of the gay, exciting life of Hollywood, died tragically Sunday. Her body was found nude in bed, a probable suicide. She was 36. The long-troubled star clutched a telephone in one hand. An empty bottle of sleeping pills was nearby.
> **Associated Press report, August 6, 1962**

61. Of course, the same could be said of many gods and goddesses, including Jesus of Nazareth himself. Jesus, too, has a history as an iconic, representative character—but that's another story.

The image of Marilyn lying on the bed, her hand clasping the telephone, speaks to us.[62] She is the ultimate signifier of the speech act at death. Her hand clasps the phone with no one at the other end. She leaves no note. Writing is dead: dead letters. The impossibility of connection under post-modernism. Did she try to reach someone? Was this pose staged? Why was she clasping the phone? Did she want to speak to us from beyond the grave, beyond death? Did she want to remind us all of the tenuous links between us? Did she want to leave a message?

Post Crypt

> I want my fans to know that I did not kill myself, and I did not take all the pills I was supposed to that day. In fact, I was trying to clean up my act with the help of my analyst. . . . I was eliminated by those who I loved and adored. I gave to a President all of my body and my very little brain. I gave to his brother all of this plus the little girl in me. I thought he loved me as 'Norma Jean' and not 'Marilyn.' And with the law that binds my spirit I was given permission to whisper in your ear all that I know and all that I can remember.
> **The spirit of Marilyn Monroe, July 16, 1990,**
> **in *The Murder of Marilyn Monroe***

It seems that Marilyn did want to leave a message. In this case, the medium gives the message or, rather, the "media," since her spirit allegedly contacted Fresno, California psychics, who have written yet another true, final account of Marilyn's last days and death, *The Murder of*

---

62. "We have felt the parasitical inclusion of a crypt, always double and doubling, duplicitous like the ear, inhabiting the haunted telephone, operating the speaking automaton which was, in the case of Frankenstein, a monument to an impossible mourning. . . . Whatever the maze of interpretative constructions, the point that might be recovered from these inventories of the imaginary rests on an inarticulate cut of separating, a story of disaster to which every reading of technology owes its opening impulse and projected end." Avital Ronell, *The Telephone Book: Technology, Schizophrenia, and Electric Speech* (Lincoln: University of Nebraska Press, 1989), 340–41.

Marilyn Monroe.[63] This time the authors go straight to the star for their information. Armed with their Ouija board and their psychic gifts, the authors conduct a series of interviews with Marilyn and a number of others about events surrounding her death: JFK, Peter Lawford, Marilyn's mother, and Sam Giancana are among the dead who speak in the text. Occasionally other spirits drift in. Dead letters, indeed.

In the post-mortem mode of remembering, the deaths of the subject and the author combine to create another mode of remembering best characterized as cryptographic. Now the dead themselves guide the hands of the authors across a board where letters are waiting to be turned into language. At times, the dead help the authors make sketches of those who were involved in Marilyn's death. The authors decode the messages of the dead. The dead speak, and the authors write down what they say. The authors verify that they are speaking to the right spirits by asking their addresses, and so on, then later cross-check the information they receive from the spirits, ascertaining that they are not talking to ghost imposters. The authors assure us that they, too, are not imposters. A long preface details the many instances of psychic contact with the beyond throughout the ages. They further assure us that they were drawn to the work only because they were contacted by the dead Marilyn. They are writing the book because "Marilyn's soul cried out for justice." If Marilyn doesn't get a chance to set the record straight, she won't be able to move on.

But what sort of message does Marilyn's spirit have for its reader? It seems that all the spirits in the book have been curiously influenced by the codes of mass-mediated discourse. Spirits such as that of JFK respond to some questions with "No comment." The dead Peter Lawford refutes a tabloid article, the one in which Marilyn is reported to be alive and well in Australia.[64] (It seems that even the dead track the virtual

63. Leonore Canevari, Jeanette van Wyhe, Christian Dimas, and Rachel Dimas, *The Murder of Marilyn Monroe* (New York: Carroll and Graf, 1992).

64. Ibid., 119–20. The discussion of the *Sun* article illustrates the curious status of mass-mediated knowledge in the cryptographic remembering. The authors write: "The *Sun* article reports that the Kennedy administration had Marilyn Monroe doped up and secretly transported to Australia. They kept her heavily

American through the tabloids.) Marilyn herself sounds as if she is some guest on a talk show, clumsily stumbling through her responses as she is guided by her earthly hosts. As was the case in the other modes of remembering Marilyn, the real messages are found in the disciplinings enacted on the subject by the authors, the ways in which the authors want to contain, punish, admonish, educate, control, resolve, head, and set free this female subject. Consider the following passage:

Q: Have you learned anything from this life?

MM: Don't fool around with anybody from the Kennedys!

Q: Come on, Marilyn, is that all you learned? Did you learn that it isn't right to have that many lovers?

MM: Yeah, I guess so.[65]

Somehow I don't think that this is the final lesson Marilyn learned from life, nor that it was the message she wanted to leave. My guess is that she

---

medicated and hidden to stop her from disclosing to the American public her affairs with the Kennedys. Other secret information she allegedly had on the Kennedys would have ended their political careers and could damage the Democratic party." In refutation, the spirit of Peter Lawford claims that the woman in Australia is a double who was placed by the Kennedy administration should their plan to kill the star ever surface. They went so far as to "destroy her fingerprints by burning." The authors then conclude that the article is "something they do not have to concern themselves with." (Thank goodness they weren't interviewing dead Elvis. Imagine the number of sightings with which they would have had to contend.) But why do they mention the article at all?

The authority of the mass-mediated realm goes unchallenged here; indeed, it is used as the direct source of authority in legitimating the story. From the foreword, written by Brad Steiger, we read that if we are doubtful about communication with the dead, we should remember that a fall 1988 study by the editors of *Better Homes and Gardens* "drew eighty thousand responses, with 89 percent of the respondents believing in eternal life, and 30 percent perceiving an astral realm in which spirits might reside." The text is speaking to other virtual textual residents, who create standards of authority and legitimacy *in medias res.*

65. Ibid., 102.

might say, along with Bartleby, "I would prefer not to." Then again, she left no note. Ah, Marilyn. Ah, humanity.

Post Script

After completing *American Monroe*, I viewed USA Network's *Marilyn and Bobby: Her Final Affair* on August 4, 1993. A moment toward the end of the made-for-television movie, which began by insisting that it was a fictional treatment of events in the public lives of its subjects, wonderfully illustrates the body politic that Marilyn is made to remember.[66] In this scene, Bobby doesn't want to break up with Marilyn, but he has to: his brother Jack is breathing down his neck; Hoover has him under surveillance; Hoffa is getting ready to kill or blackmail him. He's also being watched by Giancana's men. So he does break up with her, telling her "It's nothing personal, it's politics." Marilyn's indignant response to this line—"Nothing personal?!"—encapsulates the transformation of the political enacted under mass-mediated culture in our time. The movie is not about the kind of politics that rigidly insists on a realm outside of mass culture, or popular culture, or daily life. It insists that these distinctions don't work, that they are old, that they are "cop outs," that they can't accommodate a lot of people and their worlds. When Marilyn Monroe, coming from the poor background she did, is told by a powerful white male that his power over her is "nothing personal, just politics," she accuses the Kennedy brothers of a false, undemocratic privilege. She says that they have treated her like meat. She says that she'll get her revenge. The next thing the viewer knows, she is dead, killed by any number of men—FBI agents, mobsters, others. It's amazing how many powerful men want Marilyn dead in this movie.

66. The text at the beginning of the movie, the first thing the viewer sees, reads: "The following is a fictional account inspired by the public lives of Marilyn Monroe and Robert F. Kennedy." The movie was directed by Bradford May, and produced by Lorin B. Salob for USA Network as a USA Pictures Presentation.

However, when the film ends by listing the real-life ends of these men, we must wonder if the producers are somehow insinuating that Marilyn had her revenge in the form of history: Jack, Bobby, Jimmy, and Sam all died violently or disappeared. Was history revenging Marilyn? "Nothing personal, just politics" didn't do it for the fictional Marilyn in the made-for-TV movie. She believed that the personal *was* political, and that a political that called matters of the heart "nothing personal" was morally bankrupt. There seemed to be some hope in what she was saying, what this film was getting at. Then again, it was only a movie.

Store window, Los Angeles.
Photo by Jon Miller.

Index

Actors Studio (New York), 103
Adams, Henry, 56, 100–101
Advocate, 151
Alvarez, A., 158n
American political culture: citizens'
  incorporation into, 45–47; contested singular status of, 35–36,
  49, 79–80; death's absence in,
  148–49, 175; knowledge/power
  relations in, 146–48; Liberal
  Individualist identity of, 111–12;
  Madonna's representation of, 82;
  mass-mediated center of, 12–13;
  mass-mediated rememberings in,
  19, 40–44; Monroe's representation

of, 7–8, 20–22, 31–32, 35, 36,
  78–80, 106, 155; postmodern char-
  acter of, 20–21, 37–38; representa-
  tive characters in, 8–9, 10–12,
  38–39, 47–48. *See also* Mass-
  mediated rememberings
Anatomy Act of 1832 (Britain),
  158–59
Anderson, Benedict, 43n
Anderson, Janice, 4–5n
Andy Warhol (Gidal), 56
Anna Freud Center, 62n
Antonovich, Michael D., 117–18n
Arendt, Hannah, 13n, 46n
Arledge, Roone, 136–37

Photo by Anne Etheridge

S. Paige Baty is Assistant Professor of Politics and Women's Studies at Williams College. Continuing her explorations of the ways in which Marilyn is remembered in contemporary culture, Baty is curating a 1997 exhibition, "American Monroe," for the Williams College Museum of Art. She spent the 1993–94 academic year at Harvard University as a Faculty Mellon Fellow, working on her next book, *Representative Women: Unsettling Portraits of Still Lives.*

Design: Nola Burger
Index: Pat Deminna
Composition: Impressions
Text: 10.5/15 Adobe Garamond
Display: Officina
Printing and binding: Edwards Brothers